First World War
and Army of Occupation
War Diary
France, Belgium and Germany

4 DIVISION
Divisional Troops
Prince of Wales's Own (West Yorkshire Regiment)
21st Battalion Pioneers
14 June 1916 - 28 February 1919

WO95/1472/3

The Naval & Military Press Ltd
www.nmarchive.com
Published in association with The National Archives

Published by

The Naval & Military Press Ltd

Unit 10 Ridgewood Industrial Park,

Uckfield, East Sussex,

TN22 5QE England

Tel: +44 (0) 1825 749494

www.naval-military-press.com

www.nmarchive.com

This diary has been reprinted in facsimile from the original. Any imperfections are inevitably reproduced and the quality may fall short of modern type and cartographic standards.

© **Crown Copyright**
Images reproduced by permission of The National Archives, London, England, 2015.

Contents

Document type	Place/Title	Date From	Date To
Heading	WO95/1472/3		
Heading	4th Division War Diaries 21st West Yorks Joined From U.K June to December 1916		
War Diary	??	14/06/1916	15/06/1916
War Diary	Southampton	16/06/1916	16/06/1916
War Diary	Le Havre	17/06/1916	19/06/1916
War Diary	Vauchelles	20/06/1916	21/06/1916
War Diary	Bertrancourt	22/06/1916	07/07/1916
War Diary	Beaussart	08/07/1916	21/07/1916
War Diary	Authieule	22/07/1916	23/07/1916
War Diary	Winnezeele	24/07/1916	25/07/1916
War Diary	Poperinge	26/07/1916	26/07/1916
War Diary	Camp H	27/07/1916	28/07/1916
War Diary	Coppernollehoek	28/07/1916	31/07/1916
War Diary	Camp H	01/08/1916	01/08/1916
War Diary	Coppernollehoek	01/08/1916	05/08/1916
War Diary	Camp H	06/08/1916	06/08/1916
War Diary	Coppernollehoek	06/08/1916	13/08/1916
War Diary	H Camp	14/08/1916	14/08/1916
War Diary	Coppernollehoek	15/08/1916	22/08/1916
War Diary	Camp H	23/08/1916	23/08/1916
War Diary	Coppernollehoek	23/08/1916	25/08/1916
War Diary	Pioneer Camp	26/08/1916	08/09/1916
War Diary	Vlamertinghe	09/09/1916	16/09/1916
War Diary	On The March	17/09/1916	18/09/1916
War Diary	Villers Bocage	19/09/1916	25/09/1916
War Diary	Corbie	26/09/1916	26/09/1916
War Diary	Meaulte	27/09/1916	29/09/1916
War Diary	Citadel Camp	30/09/1916	10/10/1916
War Diary	Camp by Briqueterie	11/10/1916	23/10/1916
War Diary	Citadel Camp	24/10/1916	27/10/1916
War Diary	Ville Sur Ancre	28/10/1916	29/10/1916
War Diary	Fresnes	30/10/1916	31/10/1916
Heading	21st West Yorks November 1916 Vol 6		
War Diary	Fresne	01/11/1916	01/11/1916
War Diary	Pierrecourt	02/11/1916	04/12/1916
War Diary	Camp III	05/12/1916	07/12/1916
War Diary	Camp Near Combles	08/12/1916	27/12/1916
War Diary	Maurepas	28/12/1916	31/12/1916
Heading	4th Division War Diaries 21st West Yorks (Pioneers) 1917 Jan-1919 Feb		
War Diary	Maurepas	01/01/1917	09/01/1917
War Diary	Crucifix Camp Clery Road	10/01/1917	29/01/1917
War Diary	Camp Near Curlu Church	30/01/1917	20/02/1917
War Diary	Camp 117	21/02/1917	28/02/1917
War Diary	Camp 12 Chipilly	01/03/1917	02/03/1917
War Diary	Lahoussoye	03/03/1917	03/03/1917
War Diary	Talmas	04/03/1917	04/03/1917
War Diary	Gelaincourt	05/03/1917	05/03/1917
War Diary	Sibiville	06/03/1917	06/03/1917

War Diary	Savy	07/03/1917	08/03/1917
War Diary	Arras	09/03/1917	20/04/1917
War Diary	Habarcq	21/03/1917	22/03/1917
War Diary	Manin	23/03/1917	29/03/1917
War Diary	St Laurent Blangy	30/04/1917	01/06/1917
War Diary	Triangle	12/06/1917	07/09/1917
War Diary	Blairville	08/09/1917	20/09/1917
War Diary	Pheasant Camp In Proven	21/09/1917	28/09/1917
War Diary	Yser Canal Bank	28/09/1917	18/10/1917
War Diary	Chasseur Farm	19/10/1917	26/10/1917
War Diary	Chasseur Farm B 11 D 33	27/10/1917	31/10/1917
War Diary	Chasseur Farm Boesinghe	01/11/1917	08/11/1917
War Diary	Arras	09/11/1917	11/11/1917
War Diary	Tilloy	12/11/1917	07/02/1918
War Diary	Arras	08/02/1918	15/02/1918
War Diary	St Laurent Blangy	16/02/1918	28/02/1918
Heading	Pioneers 4th Div War Diary 21st Battn The West Yorkshire Regiment March 1918		
War Diary	St Laurent Blangy	01/03/1918	11/03/1918
War Diary	Arras	11/03/1918	22/03/1918
War Diary	Rifle Camp	23/03/1918	23/03/1918
War Diary	Duisans	24/03/1918	25/03/1918
War Diary	Rifle Camp	26/03/1918	30/03/1918
War Diary	St Laurent Blangy	31/03/1918	31/03/1918
Heading	4th Divisional Pioneers 21st Battalion West Yorkshire Regiment (Pioneers) April 1918		
War Diary	St Laurent Blangy	01/04/1918	07/04/1918
War Diary	Fosseux	08/04/1918	12/04/1918
War Diary	Le Cornet Bourdois	13/04/1918	14/04/1918
War Diary	Chateau De Werppe	15/04/1918	30/04/1918
War Diary	La Vallee	01/05/1918	24/08/1918
War Diary	Camblain Chatelain	25/08/1918	25/08/1918
War Diary	Framecourt	26/08/1918	26/08/1918
War Diary	Camblain L'Abbe	27/08/1918	28/08/1918
War Diary	Fosse Farm	29/08/1918	04/09/1918
War Diary	Hermin	04/09/1918	19/09/1918
War Diary	Feuchy	19/09/1918	21/09/1918
War Diary	Monchy Le Preux	22/09/1918	06/10/1918
War Diary	Dainville	07/10/1918	10/10/1918
War Diary	Bourlon Wood	11/10/1918	12/10/1918
War Diary	Escaut Doeuvres	13/10/1918	17/10/1918
War Diary	Naves	18/10/1918	24/10/1918
War Diary	Haspres	25/10/1918	01/11/1918
War Diary	Saulzoir	02/11/1918	04/11/1918
War Diary	Artres	05/11/1918	08/11/1918
War Diary	Le Triez	09/11/1918	18/11/1918
War Diary	Preseau	19/11/1918	03/01/1919
War Diary	Chapelle Lez Herlaimont (W. Charleroi)	04/01/1919	28/02/1919
Heading	4 Division Troops 4 Bn Machine Gun Corps 1918 Mar to 1919 Feb 234 Machine Gun Company 1917 July To 1918 Feb 21 Bn West Yorkshire R E (Pioneers) 1916 Jan To 1919 Feb		
Heading	4 Division Troops 4 Bn Machine Gun Corps 1918 Mar to 1919 Feb 234 Machine Gun Company 1917 July To 1918 Feb 21 Bn West Yorkshire Regt (Pioneers) 1916 Jan To 1919 Feb		

WD 95 Seam /1472 (3)

WD 95 1472/3 em /1471

4th Division

War Diaries

21st West Yorks

Joined from U.K. June to December

1916

Army Form C. 2118.

WAR DIARY
or
INTELLIGENCE SUMMARY
(Erase heading not required.)

21 W [illegible] Regt
[illegible] 4 Div

Instructions regarding War Diaries and Intelligence Summaries are contained in F.S. Regs., Part II. and the Staff Manual respectively. Title Pages will be prepared in manuscript.

Place	Date	Hour	Summary of Events and Information	Remarks and references to Appendices
[illegible]	June 14th	10 AM	Battⁿ was inspected in full marching order by Major Genl Bainbridge. Paraded full Coys. with 30 Officers — 1007 other ranks. Marched off 61 Horses — 57 mules — 8 bicycles. G.S. — 8 Limbered G.S. — 1 Officers Cart — 1 [illegible]	
	15th	4.55	10 Officers & 400 [illegible] entrained for [illegible] Overseas.	
		6.25	Second portion entrained under Major [illegible]	
		7.15	Third portion entrained under C.O.	
	16th	5 AM	[illegible] — Rail [illegible] arr 11.30 AM [illegible]	
			[illegible] on Officers [illegible] — 10 Horses, 108 [illegible]	
			had to be embarked alongside. Remainder of [illegible] on [illegible] "Princess Victoria" [illegible] on board by 6 P.M. [illegible]	
		7 PM	Transport left [illegible] followed by [illegible] [illegible]	
	17th		[illegible]	
		3.35 AM	H.M.S. [illegible] Duck [illegible] [illegible]	
			[illegible] under command of Major [illegible]	

Remainder of Battn [illegible] [illegible] (Transport)

Army Form C. 2118.

WAR DIARY
or
INTELLIGENCE SUMMARY
(Erase heading not required.)

Instructions regarding War Diaries and Intelligence Summaries are contained in F.S. Regs., Part II. and the Staff Manual respectively. Title Pages will be prepared in manuscript.

Place	Date	Hour	Summary of Events and Information	Remarks and references to Appendices
Le Havre	June 19th		Roll Call entrained for "Rue Eloise" - transportation arrived there about noon - Had dinner marched to Camp in Harfleur	
Harfleur	20th	5am	Battalion arrived & found fatigue party in Camp. G.O.C. 4th Bde goes over & inspects - & notified we entrain to-morrow morning	
	21st	8am	Inspected by Major Gen. Mr. Landon. G.O.C. received orders to move. Killed in Berlancourt after arena dinner. Arrived there 5pm - Moved into Bivouac	
Berlancourt	22		4 Officers & 200 men - Road making under Orders C.R.E. 4th Div.	
			6 Officers & 400 men to dig trenches tonight. Parties of officers proceeded to inspect trenches under guidance of R.E. Officers	
	23rd		4 Officers 250 men - Road making - 8 Officers & 400 men level trenches	
			4 Officers & 200 men - Road making - 1 Officer & 50 men arrived up at H.Qrs. Brigade at Berlancourt	
	24th		4 Officers & 200 men Road making - 11 Officers & 700 men at Bay Cy.	
	25th		11 Officers & 200 men Road making - 6 Officers & 400 men - trench digging	
	26th		11 Officers & tents Road making - Enemy dropped several shells in village of Berlancourt	

2449 Wt. W14957/M90 750,000 1/16 J.B.C. & A. Forms/C.2118/12.

WAR DIARY or INTELLIGENCE SUMMARY

Army Form C. 2118.

Place	Date	Hour	Summary of Events and Information	Remarks and references to Appendices
Bulloncourt	27th		6 Officers & 200 men Road making. — 1 R.C.O. & 12 men making Fascines. — 1 R.C.O. & 12 men loading stores at Aubencourt for ruclthing roads. — 1 R.C.O. & 12 men doing the same at MAILLY. No. 80.	
	28th		Pte. Rawson of "B" Coy died from gunshot wound received at MAILLY, at 8 P.M. 4th day of Bombardment. Heavy conditions made fast for anything in the shape of advance. — Very little reply from enemy. 4 Officers & 200 men Road making. — 1 R.C.O. & 12 men making Fascines. — 1 R.C.O. & 12 men loading. Order for tomorrow. — 1 Officer & 27 other ranks — looking up lunch. We went to RE 26th MAILLY — which they took 15 HIGH HOLBORN and 6th Ave Trenches — leaving them along the parapets ready for placing tomorrow. "Y" day — Supposed to be the last day of Heavy Bombardment. Order received at 2.45 P.M. — postponing Zero 48 hours, confirmed later by wire No.G.G.G./766/61. Sundown shells dropped into BERTRANCOURT — without doing any material damage.	
	29th		4 Officers & 110 men Road making — 1 Officer & R.C.O & 3 men wounded in action.	
	30th		6 Officers of "A" Coy — 1 Officer & "B" Coy — in 8 men on Lewis in correspondence with the advance. Heavy bombardment by enemy lines. Lean'd by reply.	

WAR DIARY or INTELLIGENCE SUMMARY

Army Form C. 2118.   21/W. Yorks

Place	Date	Hour	Summary of Events and Information	Remarks and references to Appendices
BERTRANCOURT	July 1st		"A" "B" Coys as per yesterday - Still employed in trenches. "C" Coy - 5 Officers, 198 Other ranks - in trenches - Heavy bombardment - Carrying Shells into advanced trenches. First day of Battle of the Somme. "C" Coy at Falfemont Wood — "D" Coy at Falfemont Wood.	
"	2.		"A" "B" Still in trenches — "C" Coy still in 4th Division Attack. "B" - 9 Officers & 296 men engaged with 4th Division Attack. 1 Officer wounded — 2 Other ranks killed - 7 Other ranks wounded.	
	3		"A" & "B" returned from trenches - "C" Coy, 6 Officers 166 OR working in front of 2nd line trenches - Casualties 2 killed 3 wounded - "D" Co. 1 Officer and 40 OR repairing trenches.	
	4		"A" Co. 5 Officers and 150 OR cleaning Battlefield. "B" Co. 5 Officers 151 OR repairing roads. "C" Co. 3 Officers 60 men working in front of Fontaine la TENDERLOIN. "D" Coy 1 Officer.	
	5		"A" Coy repairing roads - "C" Coy making new trenches - "D" Coy 1 Officer and 70 men forming Pats. 20 men and 100 men clearing Battlefield and digging graves at SUCRERIE Cemetery. "B" Coy repairing Trenches. Casualties 1 man wounded.	

Army Form C. 2118.

WAR DIARY
or
INTELLIGENCE SUMMARY
(Erase heading not required.)

Place	Date	Hour	Summary of Events and Information	Remarks and references to Appendices
BERTRANCOURT	July 6		A Coy repairing Roads. B and C Coy repairing Trenches. D Coy work at TENDERLOIN and clearing Battlefield R.	
	7		A Coy repairing Roads. B Coy repairing Trenches. D Co clearing Battlefield. Battalion moved at 8pm to BEAUSSART in consequence of Bivouac being flooded by delays of Rain - Working parties cancelled.	
BEAUSSART.	8		A Coy 30 Rks 120 OR repairing Roads. Remainder repairing Trenches. B.C. and part of D (Coy repairing Trenches. 20ff. 50 men D Coy clearing Battlefield. Casualties 1 killed 2 wounded.	
	9		A Coy 1 Off. and 50 men repairing Roads. Remainder repairing Trenches. B C + party D (Coy repairing Trenches. 2 Officers and 50 men D Coy clearing Battlefield. Casualty: 2/Lt. McGregor slightly wounded.	
	10		A Coy 1 Off 40 men Repairing Roads. Remainder Digging near Trench. B " repairing Trenches. C Coy digging new advanced Trench. D - repairing Trenches and clearing Battlefield	

Army Form C. 2118.

WAR DIARY
or
INTELLIGENCE SUMMARY
(Erase heading not required.)

Instructions regarding War Diaries and Intelligence Summaries are contained in F. S. Regs., Part II. and the Staff Manual respectively. Title Pages will be prepared in manuscript.

Place	Date	Hour	Summary of Events and Information	Remarks and references to Appendices
BEAUSSART	July 11		A Coy 1 Off = 40 men repairing Roads. Remainder Digging new Trench in front of D Coy. Remainder of P Coy repairing Trenches and clearing Battlefield. B and C Coy repairing Trenches. Casualty, 1 man wounded.	
	12		A Coy 1 Off = 40 men repairing Roads. Remainder work at new Trench with part of P Coy. Remainder of D Coy repairing Trenches and clearing Battlefield. B & C Coy repairing Trenches and tunnelling.	
	13		Work as yesterday.	
	14		Work as yesterday. Casualty. 1 man wounded	
	15		Work as yesterday.	
	16		Small parties at work. Remainder resting.	
	17		Work as on 15th but 1 Platoon of D Coy with A.D.A.S. working on Cattle Trenches. Casualties: 2 men wounded	
	18		A Coy 1 Off. 50 men Road making. Remainder making new line of Trenches in SUNKEN Road with part of D Coy. Remainder of D Coy repairing Cattle Tracks and clearing Battlefield. B and C Coy repairing Trenches - Tunnelling &c. Casualty: 1 Man.	

WAR DIARY
or
INTELLIGENCE SUMMARY

Army Form C. 2118.

Place	Date	Hour	Summary of Events and Information	Remarks and references to Appendices
BEAUSSART	July 19		A Coy Road making - New Trench - Dugouts. B Coy Mining at Sap 7 of King Street - Repairing Trenches C Coy mining: making dugouts in legend & Repairing Trenches D Coy Repairing Cable Tracks and Trenches. Clearing Battlefield. The Battalion was inspected by L. Genl Sir Aylmer Hunter Weston KCB, SO. (Comds VIII army Corps.)	
	July 20		A Coy Road making and Trenching. B Coy 1 Offr and 32 O.R. Mining - C Coy 2 Offrs & 48 mining. A Coy 1 Platoon repairing Cable track. Night work stopped in view of move tomorrow.	
	21		Battalion was relieved by the Northamptonshire Pioneers (12 Division) and marched at 9am to BUS-les-ARTOIS, halting there till 5pm and then proceeding to AUTHIEULE which we reached at 7pm.	
AUTHIEULE	22		6 Officers and 300 O.R. detached to assist entraining the Division at Stations DOULLENS and CANDAS. Remainder of Battalion resting.	

WAR DIARY
or
INTELLIGENCE SUMMARY

Army Form C. 2118.

Place	Date	Hour	Summary of Events and Information	Remarks and references to Appendices
AUTHIEULE	July 23		The Battalion marched to DOULLENS and entrained at 5pm proceeding to CASSELS where it marched to WINNEZEELE, arriving WINNEZEELE at 2 A.M. Transport arrived 4.30 A.M.	
WINNEZEELE	24		The Battalion rested at WINNEZEELE and the entraining detachments b.O(R and 300 o.R. rejoined having done very good work.	
	25		Battalion marched to POPERINGE and billeted there - The C.O. met the C.O. 4th COLDSTREAM Guards at Camp H and arranged relief. Six Officers and Six N.C.O.s went up to the Trenches and inspected the work to be taken over.	
POPERINGE	26		Head Qrs and D Coy marched to Camp H at COPERNOLLEHOEK. B Coy to PELISSIER Farm. A Coy to advanced billets at TROISTOURS. 19 Trucksmen and 50 O.R. joined C Coy to MACHINE GUN Farm. The R.E. PARK at PESELHOEK.	
Camp H	27		C.O. met Lt. MARTEL representing CRE in the Trenches and the work was arranged. B Coy worked at night in drainage of the PILCKEN road.	

Army Form C.2118.

WAR DIARY
or
INTELLIGENCE SUMMARY
(Erase heading not required.)

Instructions regarding War Diaries and Intelligence Summaries are contained in F. S. Regs., Part II. and the Staff Manual respectively. Title Pages will be prepared in manuscript.

Place	Date	Hour	Summary of Events and Information	Remarks and references to Appendices
Camp H	July 28		H⁴Qrs and D Coy - Drill	
			A Coy Work in Trenches N of Bridge 6.B.	
COPPERNOLLEHOEK			PILCKEM r'vd.	
			B " LANCASHIRE Farm	
			C " "	
	29		Work as on 28ᵗʰ	
	30		Sunday - 4ᵗʰ COLDSTREAMS left and we took over that sector	
			Work of advanced Companies as before	
	31		H⁴Qrs and D Coy - Drill and repairs to Roads, Drains and Bridges in camp	
			Advanced Companies working as before	
			Casualties: C Coy 675 Pte R HUME killed. 589 Cpl H MEDFORTH wounded by machine gun fire near LANCASHIRE Farm	

[signature]
LIEUT. COLONEL
COMDG. 21ST S (PIONEER) BN. W... ....ING REGT.

Army Form C. 2118.

WAR DIARY
or
INTELLIGENCE SUMMARY

(Erase heading not required.)

21 W York Regt
Vol 3

Place	Date	Hour	Summary of Events and Information	Remarks and references to Appendices
Camp H COPPERNOLLEHOEK	1916 Aug 1		A Coy - Constructing new Alleyway parallel to the Canal northwards from Huddersfield Comm. Trench.	
			B Coy - Revetting X Line East of PILCKEM Road - Widening and deepening drainage trench along East side of PILCKEM Road.	
			C Coy - Revetting X Line West of PILCKEM Road and excavating continuation to HALIFAX Road Trench. Casualty; 1 man wounded -	
			D Coy - At Rear Quarters - Drill and work improving accommodation at the Camp - and the roads -	
	Aug 2		Work the same as yesterday - Sergt HODGSON, B Company, wounded.	
	Aug 3		Same work continued.	
	Aug 4		Same work continued. Sergt GARDNER, B Company, wounded.	
	Aug 5		Same work continued	

Army Form C. 2118.

WAR DIARY
or
INTELLIGENCE SUMMARY
(Erase heading not required.)

Instructions regarding War Diaries and Intelligence Summaries are contained in F. S. Regs., Part II. and the Staff Manual respectively. Title Pages will be prepared in manuscript.

Place	Date	Hour	Summary of Events and Information	Remarks and references to Appendices
Camp at COPPER NULLEMOEK	10/6 Aug			
	Aug 7		Sunday. A, B and C Companies, same work continued – D Coy HdQts, Church Parade.	
	8		Same work continued –	
			Same work continued – In consequence of Gas Attack A, B & C Companies were withdrawn from the Trenches early – Casualties: Lt. OAKEY and one man wounded – One man Gassed –	
	9		D Coy. marched to PELISSIER Farm to relieve B Coy.	
	10		Same work continued	
	11		do	
	12		do	
	13		do	
			Casualty: 1 man, C Coy, Wounded –	

2449 Wt. W14957/Mgo 750,000 1/16 J.B.C. & A. Forms/C.2118/12.

Army Form C. 2118.

WAR DIARY
or
INTELLIGENCE SUMMARY
(Erase heading not required.)

Instructions regarding War Diaries and Intelligence Summaries are contained in F.S. Regs., Part II. and the Staff Manual respectively. Title Pages will be prepared in manuscript.

Place	Date	Hour	Summary of Events and Information	Remarks and references to Appendices
H Camp, COPPERNOLLEHOEK	1916 Aug 15		Same work continued - Casualty: 1 man wounded D Coy -	
	16		Same work continued - Casualties 1 man C.Coy - wounded 1 man A Coy - do	
	17		do	
	18		do	
	19		A and C Companies continued work - D Co stopped for move.	
	20		A and C Companies moved from TROISTOURS to Camp F D Coy moved from PELISSIER to Head Quarters -	
	21		Sunday - Church Parade at MP Gyr -	
	22		Companies resting and working in Camp do	

2449 Wt. W14957/M90 750,000 1/16 J.B.C. & A. Forms/C.2118/12.

WAR DIARY or INTELLIGENCE SUMMARY

Army Form C. 2118.

Place	Date	Hour	Summary of Events and Information	Remarks and references to Appendices
Camp H GOPPEANOLLEHOEK	1916 Aug 23		Companies resting and working in camp.	
	24		B, C and D companies march to Infantry Barracks YPRES to relieve 3rd Canadian Pioneers in Salient.	
	25		B Coy took up work in RITZ TRENCH rt in KIRBY STREET making deep tre'ing trench with Dugouts and a main drain. C " " " " D Coy similar work in FORT STREET.	
PIONEER Camp	26		Head Qrs and A Company marched to PIONEER Camp, 2½ miles East of YPRES. B C and D continued work as yesterday. At 9 AM the enemy bombarded front line heavily lifting at about 9:30 AM on to KIRBY Street in which 2/Lt Wood was at work with 50 men. This trench was except	

Army Form C. 2118.

WAR DIARY
or
INTELLIGENCE SUMMARY

(Erase heading not required.)

Instructions regarding War Diaries and Intelligence Summaries are contained in F. S. Regs., Part II. and the Staff Manual respectively. Title Pages will be prepared in manuscript.

Place	Date	Hour	Summary of Events and Information	Remarks and references to Appendices
PIONEER Camp	1916 Aug 26		in three places for a length of 50 yards, rendering it very difficult to reconstruct. Casualties: 2 men killed; 14 wounded.	
	27		Work continued as yesterday.	
	28		do A Coy 50 men took up work at HILL 60.	
	29		do but much interfered with by deluge	
	30		do of Rain. Trenches flooded.	
	31		Work continued as before.	

4 Sept. 1916

S.H.A. Markham
LIEUT. COLONEL
COMDG. 21ST (PIONEER) BN WEST YORKS REGT.

Army Form C. 2118.

21 W York Regt.

WAR DIARY
or
INTELLIGENCE SUMMARY
(Erase heading not required.)

Place	Date	Hour	Summary of Events and Information	Remarks and references to Appendices
PIONEER CAMP.	1916 Sept 1.		A Company to Hand Qrs for Drill and Training.	
			B " at Belgian Infantry Barracks, Ypres, working on Rifle Trench and widening Tunnellers at Mount Sorrel.	
			C " to Head Quarters for Drill and Training.	
			D " at Belgian Infantry Barracks YPRES working in FORT St and SANDGATE Rd Winter work of A and C Companies to Pioneers of 1st Australian Division.	
	2)		B and D Companies moved from Belgian Infantry Barracks to other Billets in YPRES. One Platoon occupied a part of the CLOTH HALL and the rest of B Co. the Church of a Convent. D Co's partly in Cellars and partly in the Halls of a Convent. These billets being very much exposed, had to be protected with heavy shell proof cover on which a proportion of both Companies was occupied during the whole time B Co. remained in YPRES. By the time they left very good and safe Shell proof billets had been made. Sanitary arrangements, Water in places and Latrines constructed — and the economics made clean and wholesome.	

WAR DIARY or INTELLIGENCE SUMMARY

Army Form C. 2118.

(Erase heading not required.)

Place	Date	Hour	Summary of Events and Information	Remarks and references to Appendices
PIONEER CAMP.	9/16 Sept 3		B and D Companies at work in Trenches and on Shell Proof over Billets. A and C at drill and training at H.Qrs.	
	4		Work as above –	
	5		do –	
	6		do – 2nd LAMBTON inspected Billets of Companies in YPRES.	
	7		do – Took over work in 29th Division Area –	
	8		A Company moved from H.Qrs. to PELLISIER Farm for work in Trenches in 38th Division Area –	
	9		do –	
	10		C Coy from 112 Qr. to L.E. WORKS –	
	11		Head Qrs. from PIONEER Camp to VLAMERTINGHE CHATEAU. Transport and H.Qr. Coy from PIONEER Camp to hutts near BRANDHOEK. B and D Companies handed over their work in Trenches to PIONEER Battn of 2nd Australian Division.	
	12		Took over work for A and C Companies in 38th Division Area.	

Army Form C. 2118.

WAR DIARY
or
INTELLIGENCE SUMMARY
(Erase heading not required.)

Place	Date	Hour	Summary of Events and Information	Remarks and references to Appendices
VLAMERTINGHE	1915 Sept 9		A Company commenced reconstruction of BARNSLEY (CANAL) Road. C Company having taken over work in HALIFAX and HUDDERSFIELD Communication Trenches yesterday had it cancelled last night. Other work was allotted to them today in THREADNEEDLE Street and GOWTHORPE Rd. They lost a day's work in trenches, but were usefully employed in improving their Billets.	
	10		B and D Companies commenced work reconstructing the KAAIE SALIENT line in front of YPRES.	
	11		Work as above.	
			do. Casualty: D Coy, 1 man wounded.	
	12		do	
	13		do	
	14		do	
	15		do Casualty: B Coy, 1 man wounded.	
	16		Orders received to concentrate and move with IV Division. Work stopped and preparations made for the move.	

Army Form C. 2118.

WAR DIARY
or
INTELLIGENCE SUMMARY

(Erase heading not required.)

Instructions regarding War Diaries and Intelligence Summaries are contained in F. S. Regs., Part II. and the Staff Manual respectively. Title Pages will be prepared in manuscript.

Place	Date	Hour	Summary of Events and Information	Remarks and references to Appendices
In the March	1916 Sept 17		Battalion concentrated at 10 AM at Camp 7 near St Sixte) marching from the various Billets round YPRES. Proceeded at 2 PM to entrain at PROVEN and was inspected en route by Lt Genl Sir AYLMER HUNTER-WESTON commanding VIII Corps who wished it success on leaving his command – Entrained and left PROVEN at 5 pm; via CALAIS, BOULOGNE and ABBEVILLE	
do	18		Arrived LONGUEAU, S.E. of AMIENS, 7.30 AM and marched to VILLERS BOCAGE where it was billeted with Divisional HQrs. 2nd Division. Very heavy Rain.	
VILLERS -BOCAGE	19		Inspection of Arms and Ammunition – drying clothing etc	
	20		Issue made here of new Box Respirators, made instead of one for a Helmet – Instruction of Officers & NCO's and fitting of Respirators –	
	21		Battalion employed at Physical Drill, Bayonet fighting and Bombing –	
	22		do	
	23		do	
	24		Sunday – Church Parade and a Cross Country Race –	
	25		Battalion marched to CORBIE and was in Billets there for the night	

WAR DIARY
or
INTELLIGENCE SUMMARY
(Erase heading not required.)

Army Form C. 2118.

Place	Date	Hour	Summary of Events and Information	Remarks and references to Appendices
CORBIE	Sept 1916 26		In consequence of the Division not going to the front immediately the Battalion was lent to the XIV Corps. The C.O. went to H.Q.s for instructions from the Chief Engineer and the Battalion marched to MÉAULTE and billeted there.	
MÉAULTE	27		2nd Officers and 100 men B Coy under Captain SAMPSON marched to CITADEL Camp to work at PLATEAU Station. This Camp was Bombed by Aircraft at night and one man was wounded (Pte M NALLY).	
	28		A Company employed Striking Camps in Happy Valley and erecting Camp near MAMETZ. Work as above. C and D Companies also employed in MÉAULTE	
	29		Handed over work to SEAFORTH Highlrs. Battalion moved to CITADEL Camp on a very wet morning and much of bad Camp got. 450 men at work for C.E. XIV Corps.	
CITADEL Camp	30		Working parties, Drill and Fatigues.	

4 Oct. 1916

[signature]

Army Form C. 2118.

21 W Yorks Regt

Vol 5

WAR DIARY
or
INTELLIGENCE SUMMARY
(Erase heading not required.)

Instructions regarding War Diaries and Intelligence Summaries are contained in F. S. Regs., Part II. and the Staff Manual respectively. Title Pages will be prepared in manuscript.

Place	Date	Hour	Summary of Events and Information	Remarks and references to Appendices
CITADEL CAMP	Oct 1. 1916		Sunday. Church Parade. 2 Companies working for C.E. XIV Corps.	
	2		All available men at work for C.E. XIV Corps. Heavy Rain.	
	3		ditto - work impeded by state of the ground.	
	4		ditto Heavy Rain.	
	5		ditto C Company, under Major Bamford, attached to XIV Corps Pioneer Group.	
	6		All available men working for C.E. XIV Corps.	
	7	9 A.M.	All available men working for C.E. XIV Corps.	
	8	7 A.M.	Rejoined IV Division in the evening.	
	9		Camps inspected by General Lambton. Refreshments Music.	
	10		Marched to Camp near Ponquevillers, relieving the Cheshire Pioneer Battalion.	

Army Form C. 2118.

WAR DIARY
or
INTELLIGENCE SUMMARY
(Erase heading not required.)

Instructions regarding War Diaries and Intelligence Summaries are contained in F. S. Regs., Part II. and the Staff Manual respectively. Title Pages will be prepared in manuscript.

Place	Date	Hour	Summary of Events and Information	Remarks and references to Appendices
Camp/ 04 BRUETERNE	1916 Oct 11		Took up new work on Roads &c.	
		12	D Company working on communications — A and B at night with the front line — A with Durham R.E. working for 12th Brigade. B, with 9 Field Coy R.E., working for 10th Brigade — Casualties B, one man killed, two wounded.	
			B Coy, two men killed, two wounded. An attack by 10th and 12th Brigades took place this afternoon to establish a line in advance of existing position, but was not entirely successful — the work done by the companies was to consolidate the portion of position gained —	
		13	D Coy on communications work. A + B in the line at night.	
		14	do	
			A raft attempt was made to secure certain points by the outside and B Coy was out all night but not actually at work. They had one man wounded.	

Army Form C. 2118.

WAR DIARY
or
INTELLIGENCE SUMMARY
(Erase heading not required.)

Place	Date	Hour	Summary of Events and Information	Remarks and references to Appendices
Camp by BRUAY BRIE	15 Oct		A Coy working on new Trenches in front line of the 12th Bde front. B Coy working on new Trenches of front line of the 16th Bde front. D Coy working on Communications -	
	Oct 16		A Coy on new Trench in front line of left Brigade - B Coy resting D Coy on Communications -	
	17		B Coy preparing shelters in SERPENTINE and TATLER Trenches which they occupied during the night to support an attack the following morning. A and D Companies resting -	
	18		D Company marched to join B Company in Trenches arriving there at 4.30 A.M. These Companies here heavily shelled. The objective was not gained by the 12th Infantry Brigade and B Coy returned to Camp at 10 A.M. D Coy remained in the trenches. Casualties Lieut HUCKLEBRIDGE, Coy Sgt Major SHAW and 5 men wounded.	

WAR DIARY or INTELLIGENCE SUMMARY

Army Form C. 2118.

Place	Date 1916	Hour	Summary of Events and Information	Remarks and references to Appendices
Camp by SANCTERIE	Oct 18		(Continued) On this night A Coy, which had been in reserve in Camp, dug 214 yards of trench from Ox Trench to SUSSEX Road. B Coy dug a communication trench from ANTELOPE trench to ANDREWS POST in advance of the front line of right Brigade. D Coy dug a communication trench to front line of left Brigade. During this work Corporal Howarth and 4 men were killed — Pte HUGHES was missing; and Corporal RUBERY and 5 men were wounded — 2/Lieut LINK was injured by turning to shelter.	
	19		All Companies resting; work being cancelled in consequence of very heavy rain.	
	20		B and D Companies excavating fire trench from BURNABY trench to ANDREWS POST on front of Right Brigade. C Coy rejoined from GRAND FLEET FRONT EXTENSION TRENCH. A Coy in reserve. 1 Man wounded	

Army Form C. 2118.

WAR DIARY
or
INTELLIGENCE SUMMARY

(Erase heading not required.)

Instructions regarding War Diaries and Intelligence Summaries are contained in F. S. Regs., Part II. and the Staff Manual respectively. Title Pages will be prepared in manuscript.

Place	Date	Hour	Summary of Events and Information	Remarks and references to Appendices
Camp nr BRIQUETERIE	Oct 1916	21	A and C Companies widening and improving Communication Trench between OX trench and MUGGY trench. Casualties Captain ADAMSON, Sgt HARTLEY and one man wounded. B Coy widening and deepening GERMAN CHORD trench and Coy completing trench from BURNABY trench to ANDREWS POST. D Coy completing trench from BURNABY trench to ANDREWS POST. Casualties 1 man killed and 4 wounded.	
		22	A and B Companies traced out lines near front line trench from WINDY to BURNABY trench in Left Brigade Sector — the work was very well done as Sappers learning, working from each end. Casualties Captain E. BOULNOIS killed and Captain G.S. NOON and Sergeant BUSH severely wounded. C Coy making new trench in front of GERMAN CHORD, night. Brigade Sector. Casualties Lieut E. OAKEY and 3 men wounded. D Coy Cable trench	

Army Form C. 2118.

WAR DIARY
or
INTELLIGENCE SUMMARY
(Erase heading not required.)

Place	Date	Hour	Summary of Events and Information	Remarks and references to Appendices
Camp by BRIQUETERIE	1916 Oct 23		Work in front line was completed last night – General LAMBTON Commanding 4th Division visited the Camp and addressed the Battalion, expressing his satisfaction with their work – The Battalion marched at 2 pm to the CITADEL Camp, leaving C Company for duty with the XIV Corps PIONEER group in camp at MONTAUBAN.	
CITADEL Camp	Oct 24		Resting at CITADEL Camp	
"	25		ditto – Very heavy Rain –	
"	26		Company training.	
"	27		The Battalion, less C Company, marched to VILLE SUR ANCRE and went into Billets –	

Army Form C. 2118.

WAR DIARY
or
INTELLIGENCE SUMMARY
(Erase heading not required.)

Instructions regarding War Diaries and Intelligence Summaries are contained in F. S. Regs., Part II. and the Staff Manual respectively. Title Pages will be prepared in manuscript.

Place	Date 1916	Hour	Summary of Events and Information	Remarks and references to Appendices
VILLE SUR ANCRE.	Oct 28		Rest.	
	29		The Battalion, less C Company, marched at 12.15pm to MÉRICOURT and entrained for AIRESNES which was reached at Midnight. The transport left at 6 AM and proceeded by road to ARQUEUVRES.	
FRESNES	30		Battalion marched to FRESNES about 11 miles and went into Billets, the Transport arriving at 8 pm.	
	31		Rest.	

A.P.Watts Lieut. COLONEL
COMDG. 21st (PIONEER) Bn. WEST YORKS REGT.

ORDERLY ROOM
31-10-16
21st S. (PIONEER) Bn. W. YORKS REGT.

Pub 6.

21st West Fork 8.

November 1916.

Army Form C. 2118.

WAR DIARY
or
INTELLIGENCE SUMMARY
(Erase heading not required.)

Instructions regarding War Diaries and Intelligence Summaries are contained in F. S. Regs., Part II. and the Staff Manual respectively. Title Pages will be prepared in manuscript.

Place	Date	Hour	Summary of Events and Information	Remarks and references to Appendices
FRESNE Moy	1916		The Battalion (less C Company) marched from FRESNE to PIERRECOURT and went into Billets.	
PIERRECOURT.	2		Settled into Billets and arranged work.	
	3		Company Training	
	4		do	
	5		Church Parade	
	6		General Inspection by M.G. 4th Division inspected.	
	7		Company training	
	8		do	
	9th to 16th }		C Company rejoined from XIV Corps, under Major H. B. ADAMSON. Deaths of Captain H.B. HOAMSON from wounds received on 21st October upheld, having occurred on 30th October —	
	30th }		Company training —	

J.M.R.Marke

3 Dec 1916.

2449 Wt. W14957/M90 750,000 1/16 J.B.C. & A. Forms/C.2118/12.

Army Form C. 2118.

21 W. York Regt
Vol 7

WAR DIARY
or
INTELLIGENCE SUMMARY
(Erase heading not required.)

Instructions regarding War Diaries and Intelligence Summaries are contained in F.S. Regs., Part II. and the Staff Manual respectively. Title Pages will be prepared in manuscript.

Place	Date 1916	Hour	Summary of Events and Information	Remarks and references to Appendices
PIERRECOURT	Dec 1		Orders received for move.	
	2		General LAMBTON, cmg 4th Division, inspected – Transport marched out 1PM for WOIREL.	
	3		Church Parade and preparations for move –	
	4		Left PIERRECOURT at 5 hrs; entrained at OISEMONT alg 7AM and arrived EDGEHILL 1PM. Marched to Camp 111 near BRAY.	
CAMP 111	5&6		Remained in Camp – General LAMBTON visited.	
	7		"A" Coy proceeded to camp near COMBLES.	
Camp near COMBLES	8		Remainder of Battalion marched to new Camp – Working out dugouts, ice on modestion being quite hard spate	
	9		Took up work in the line – "A" Coy Shelton Government in French	
	10		"B" Coy Northern communication trench & "D" Coy working on Roads in front of COMBLES – casualties, one man wounded.	

Army Form C. 2118.

WAR DIARY
or
INTELLIGENCE SUMMARY

(Erase heading not required.)

Instructions regarding War Diaries and Intelligence Summaries are contained in F. S. Regs., Part II. and the Staff Manual respectively. Title Pages will be prepared in manuscript.

Place	Date	Hour	Summary of Events and Information	Remarks and references to Appendices
Cunfrecourt COMBLES	Dec	11	Work as yesterday — One man killed.	
		12	do	
		13	A and B Companies as before. C Coy working under orders of the 6th Field Coy R.E. and D Coy with 12th Brigade.	
		14	Work as yesterday.	
		15	Work as yesterday.	
		16	Work as yesterday.	
		17	At 4.45 A.M a heavy shell fell in B Coy's dugouts killing Cpl/m/Sgt Hartley, Sergt France and Pte Hartley; and wounding seven men — Work as yesterday.	
		18	Work as yesterday. Casualties: 5 men wounded. —	
		19	do	
		20	do	
		21	do	Casualties: 2 men wounded. —
		22	do	1 man killed: 4 wounded. —

WAR DIARY
or
INTELLIGENCE SUMMARY
(Erase heading not required.)

Army Form C. 2118.

Place	Date	Hour	Summary of Events and Information	Remarks and references to Appendices
Camp near COMBLES	Dec 23		Work as before – Casualties: 2 men wounded –	
	24		Work as before – 2 men wounded –	
	25		do	
	26		"C" Company moved in advance Party to Camp MAUREPAS Ravine. Work as before that C Coy were employed making good the new Camp and improving. "B" reports to MAUREPAS every day	
	27		9th Field Company R.E. Battalion moved to Camp MAUREPAS RAVINE.	
MAUREPAS	28		Work as above.	
	29		Work as above. A and B Coy on BETTYS SUPPORT – 1 man wounded	
	30		Trench had work in 15th life – do	
	31		Sunday –	

J.H.V. Franks

4th Division

War Diaries

21st West Yorks (PIONEERS)

~~January~~ to ~~December~~
~~1917~~

1917 JAN — 1919 FEB

Instructions regarding War Diaries and Intelligence Summaries are contained in F. S. Regs., Part II. and the Staff Manual respectively. Title Pages will be prepared in manuscript.

WAR DIARY
or
~~INTELLIGENCE SUMMARY~~
(Erase heading not required.)

Army Form C. 2118.

21 W York Regt

Vol 8

4

Place	Date	Hour	Summary of Events and Information	Remarks and references to Appendices
MAUREPAS	1917 Jan	1	[illegible] erecting camps of NISSEN Huts under XV Corps [illegible]	
			C and D [illegible] Intermediate Trench from FREGICOURT to RANCOURT.	
			Small parties [illegible] in Camp [illegible] for R.E.	
		2	As above	
		3	do	
		4	do	
		5	A [illegible] NISSEN Huts [illegible]	
			C [illegible] D as above	
		6	A [illegible] Camps of NISSEN huts [illegible]	
			D on Intermediate Line.	
		7	A [illegible] NISSEN Huts. B Coy moved to Camp [illegible] on [illegible] Road.	
			C [illegible] Intermediate Line	
			This day was [illegible] to be kept as [illegible]	
			[illegible] the Battalion [illegible] employed [illegible]	
		8	A, C [illegible] D [illegible] HUTS. A and D moved to [illegible] Camp	
			C [illegible] R.E.	
		9	As above. [illegible]	

2449 Wt. W14957/M90 750,000 1/16 J.B.C. & A. Forms/C.2118/12.

Army Form C. 2118.

WAR DIARY
or
INTELLIGENCE SUMMARY

(Erase heading not required.)

Instructions regarding War Diaries and Intelligence Summaries are contained in F. S. Regs., Part II. and the Staff Manual respectively. Title Pages will be prepared in manuscript.

Place	Date	Hour	Summary of Events and Information	Remarks and references to Appendices
CRUCIFIX CORNER CLERY RD.	Jan 10		as before	
	11		do	
	12		do	
	13		do	
	14		Sent 2 officers and D.S.O.R. Ranks to Bois L'Abbé for fatigue Building work with C.R.E.	
	15		C Company rejoined H.Q. 1 Sergeant, 1 Corporal & — D Coy	
	16		A & B on NISSEN Huts and Camp – C & D on CLERY Road.	
	17		as above	
	18		A & B as above and preparing dugouts for new CURLU CHURCH C & D on communication trenches.	
	19		as above – D Coy making Mule track CLERY to BOUCHAVESNES.	
	20		as above	
	21		A & B Coy work on Mixed Dugouts and new coleworks C on communication trenches. D on mule track improving it for wheeled transport	
	22		as above. C Coy moved to JUNCTION Wood	
	23		do do B Coy on NISSEN huts	

2449 Wt. W14957/M90 750,000 1/16 J.B.C. & A. Forms/C.2118/12.

WAR DIARY or INTELLIGENCE SUMMARY

Army Form C. 2118.

(Erase heading not required.)

Place	Date	Hour	Summary of Events and Information	Remarks and references to Appendices
CRUCIFIX CORNER	1917 Sept 24		Work as before.	
CLERY RAVINE	25		do.	
	26		do. 2 Companys moved 2 Platoons to JUNCTION ROAD, 1 Platoon to MARRIERES WOOD	
	27		as. Remainder Platoon of D Co. to JUNCTION WOOD.	
			Bty to camp near CURLU CHURCH to prepare for Battalion move	
	28		A Coy on intrench dugouts #2	
			B " preparing camp. C Coy. Communication Trenches.	
			D " Starting Quarterplug of Dugouts at MARRIERES Wood.	
	29		Work as above.	
Camp near CURLU CHURCH.	30		do. C Coy excavating loop trench out of LADDER AVENUE	
	31		Headqrs moved to Nr Camp front of BOUCHAVESNE.	
			In the am yesterday	
			Casualty. A Coy. 1 man wounded -	

J.W.H. Janke
LIEUT. COLONEL
21st (PIONEERS) Bn. WEST YORKS REGT.

Army Form C. 2118.

WAR DIARY
or
INTELLIGENCE SUMMARY

21 W York R[?]

(Erase heading not required.)

Instructions regarding War Diaries and Intelligence Summaries are contained in F. S. Regs., Part II. and the Staff Manual respectively. Title Pages will be prepared in manuscript.

Place	Date	Hour	Summary of Events and Information	Remarks and references to Appendices
CAMP nr CORLU CHURCH	Feb 1 1917		A and B Co's in huts in rest camp and improvements to the lines. C Ladder Communication trench and new steps in front of BOUCHEVESNES. D Coy making Splinter Proof Shelter in MARRIERES Wood.	Map Sh. 9
	2		Work as above but 1 Platoon of D Co on new Railway Track nr MARRIERES Wood.	
	3		Work as yesterday.	
	4		C Coy working with D on new Railway Track. Constructing other loop on LADDER Communication Trench A & B Companies change with C & D.	
	5		Work as yesterday. A & B Companies relieved C & D.	
	6		Maintenance of Communication Trenches. Making Splinter Proof Dug-outs. Moved Dug-outs. Supply Decauville Railways.	
	7		A Coy Dug-outs nr MARRIERES Wd. B Coy New Road ANDOVER PLACE to Tn of MARRIERES Wood. C " in Camp D " Salvaging Trench HENDLEIT North and working on TWL CLERY BETHLEHEM DUMP	Casualty 1 man wounded
	8		As above - D Coy extending Decauville Railway to ANDOVER PLACE.	Casualty 1 man wounded.

2449 Wt. W14957/M90 750,000 1/16 J.B.C. & A. Forms/C.2118/12.

Army Form C. 2118.

WAR DIARY
or
INTELLIGENCE SUMMARY

(Erase heading not required.)

Instructions regarding War Diaries and Intelligence Summaries are contained in F. S. Regs., Part II. and the Staff Manual respectively. Title Pages will be prepared in manuscript.

Place	Date	Hour	Summary of Events and Information	Remarks and references to Appendices
Camp near CURLU CHURCH	Feb 9	10	Work as yesterday. "C" Coy salvaging Mining Rds -	
		11	do. do.	
		12	do. - Casualty 1 man wounded -	
		13	do. - All Companies at work -	
		14	D Company moved from Camp to Junction Wood. Work as yesterday. Orders received to erase work up to & by and concentrate on the pulling of LADDER and LONDON trenches in front of BOUCHEVESNES up to Support lines. — Casualty 1 man wounded	
		15	Works thro' next night. A & C Coy LONDON Avenue — B and D Coy LADDER Avenue. C Company moved from Camp to MARRIERES Wood Dugouts. Men began todays and work became very difficult — No moon at night and said ice locust about 3 inches of slush — Hard work and very little progress to shew.	

WAR DIARY
or
INTELLIGENCE SUMMARY

Army Form C. 2118.

Place	Date	Hour	Summary of Events and Information	Remarks and references to Appendices
CAMP near CURLU CHURCH	Feb 1917 16		Work continued as yesterday under great difficulties	
	17		do - Owing to fog it was possible to do more work by day; with better results. Casualty: 1 man wounded.	
	18		do - Trenches becoming flooded and requiring constant pumping - Casualties: 2 men wounded	
	19		do - All Companies concentrated at H.Qrs and marched over to 8th Division	
Camp 117	20			
	21		Battalion moved to Camp 117 on BRAY-CORBIE Road	
	22		Battalion moved to Camp 12 near CHIPILLY	
	23		Resting and improving Camp. Reinforcement of 65 O.R. joined.	
	24		do	
	25		Sunday	
	26		Company training	
	27		and Musketry	
	28			

[Signed] Lieut. Colonel
COMDG. 21ST (PIONEER) BN. WEST YORKS REGT.

Army Form C. 2118.

WAR DIARY
or
INTELLIGENCE SUMMARY
(Erase heading not required.)

2/1 W. York Regt
1 of 10

Place	Date	Hour	Summary of Events and Information	Remarks and references to Appendices
Camp 12	1917 March 1		Company training and Musketry.	
CHIPILLY	2		do	
"	3		Marched at 10 AM, under orders received during the night, to LAHOUSSOYE and billeted there.	
LAHOUSSOYE	4		Marched at 8.30 AM to THOMAS.	
THOMAS	5		Marched at 8.30 AM to GEZAINCOURT.	
GEZAINCOURT	6		Marched at 8.30 AM via DOULLENS to SIBIVILLE.	
SIBIVILLE	7		Marched at 8.30 AM to SAVY and reported for duty to Chief Engineers XVII Corps at AUBIGNY.	
SAVY	8		Marched at 8.30 AM A and B Companies to ETRUN and took over work from Pioneer Battn. NORTHUMBERLAND Fusiliers. Head Quarters and C and D Companies to Marched at 4 PM. from Pioneer Battn. ROYAL SCOTS - ARRAS and took over work from St CATHERINE and St NICHOLAS	
ARRAS	9		Work under XVII Corps at ETRUN and St CATHERINE and St NICHOLAS	
	10		do	
	11		do	
	12		do	

Army Form C. 2118.

WAR DIARY
or
INTELLIGENCE SUMMARY
(Erase heading not required.)

Instructions regarding War Diaries and Intelligence Summaries are contained in F. S. Regs., Part II. and the Staff Manual respectively. Title Pages will be prepared in manuscript.

Place	Date	Hour	Summary of Events and Information	Remarks and references to Appendices
ARRAS	March 13		Work under XVII Corps at ETRUN, St CATHERINE and ST NICHOLAS.	
	14		do	
	15		do	
	16		do	
	17		do	
	18		do	
	19		do	
	20		do Casualty: 1 man wounded. Reinforcements arrived 82.	
	21		do	
	22		do	
	23		do Reinforcements arrived 38	
	24		do	
	25		do	
	26		do	
	27		do Casualties: 2 men wounded.	
	28		do	

2449 Wt. W14957/M90 750,000 1/16 J.B.C. & A. Forms/C.2118/12.

WAR DIARY
or
INTELLIGENCE SUMMARY
(Erase heading not required.)

Army Form C. 2118.

Place	Date	Hour	Summary of Events and Information	Remarks and references to Appendices
ARRAS	1917 March 30		Work under XVII Corps at ETRUN, St CATHERINE and St NICHOLAS	
	31		do. Casualties; 4 men killed. 2/Lt Richardson and 4 men wounded.	
			do.	

G.M.Parke
LIEUT. COLONEL
COMDG 21ST S. PIONEER Bⁿ. WEST YORKS REG^t.

Army Form C. 2118.

21 W York Regt.
XI

WAR DIARY
or
INTELLIGENCE SUMMARY
(Erase heading not required.)

Instructions regarding War Diaries and Intelligence Summaries are contained in F. S. Regs., Part II. and the Staff Manual respectively. Title Pages will be prepared in manuscript.

Place	Date	Hour	Summary of Events and Information	Remarks and references to Appendices
ARRAS	1917 April 1		Strength on this date 38 Officers 981 O.R. Work under XVII Corps at ÉTRUN, St CATHERINE and St NICHOLAS preparing roads and tramways for advance.	
	2		do Casualty: 1 man wounded. D Coy.	
	3		do " 3 men wounded. C Coy.	
	4		do 2/Lt Grayjones Concussion. Corpl GOTT killed - 1 man wounded. D Coy	
	5		do " 2 men wounded. C. Coy, D Coy.	
	6		do " 2 men wounded. C and D Coy.	
	7		do " 1 man wounded.	
	8		do	
	9		Battle of ARRAS. A and B Companies extending light Railways from ROCKINCOURT to old GERMAN line towards NINE ELMS. C Coy making BAILLEUL Road passable for Guns and wheel traffic over BRITISH Line and NO MANS LAND up to COMMERCE CRATER - D Coy making St LAURENCE-BLANGY Road similarly towards from the BRITISH Line, over No Mans Land and the GERMAN line to St LAURENCE BLANGY church. The advance began at 5.30 AM speed was so successful that the Companies under commence work	

2449 Wt. W14957/M90 750,000 1/16 J.B.C. & A. Forms/C.2118/12.

Army Form C. 2118.

WAR DIARY
or
INTELLIGENCE SUMMARY

(Erase heading not required.)

Instructions regarding War Diaries and Intelligence Summaries are contained in F. S. Regs., Part II. and the Staff Manual respectively. Title Pages will be prepared in manuscript.

Place	Date	Hour	Summary of Events and Information	Remarks and references to Appendices
ARRAS	April 18	9	At 7.30 A.M. with very little interference from the enemy fired on the vicinity	
			Coys called home to men wounded.	
		10	Work as above.	
		11	Work as above. Also Transport and Gymnastic from 8pm Y huts into tents.	
		12	Work as above.	
		13	A + B Companies w/l sent back to Wholo Barnham Camp in light to	
			A.R.E and worked together on the S LAURENT BLANGY Road to free us	
			the Railway Embankment.	
		14	Work as above.	
		15	do	
		16	Took up rest work with B Coy and work from S LAURENT BLANGY to BLANGY. The	
			other Companies working as before. Casualty 2 men wounded -	
		17	Work as above. Casualty Serj. Provost A Coy wounded.	
		18	A Coy working on Cross Road, A Thies to GRAVILLE Road. B Coy as before. Cross Road from	
			A Thies to Point du Jour, Band C as before. Casualty 2 men wounded -	
		19	A and B Coys on the same roads, came upon A.A box type of dead burial there	
			not yet been identified - Sent Monthly and Biweekly reports in.	

2449 Wt. W14957/M90 750,000 1/16 J.B.C. & A. Forms/C.2118/12.

WAR DIARY
or
INTELLIGENCE SUMMARY
(Erase heading not required.)

Army Form C. 2118.

Instructions regarding War Diaries and Intelligence Summaries are contained in F. S. Regs., Part II. and the Staff Manual respectively. Title Pages will be prepared in manuscript.

Place	Date	Hour	Summary of Events and Information	Remarks and references to Appendices
ARRAS	1917 April 20		A and B Coy on Road from St LAURENCE BLANGY to BLANGY - C and D in front from St NICHOLAS OILWORKS through St LAURENCE BLANGY. Handed over work to 1/8th Royal Scots on relief and rejoined the 42nd Division after six weeks work under the XVII Corps -	
HABARCQ	21		Marched at 10 AM to HABARCQ and went into Billets for rest.	
	22		Sunday - At HABARCQ.	
	23		Marched at 10 AM to MANIN	
MANIN	24 25 26 27		Resting at MANIN	
	28		Marched at 9 AM to Y Huts	
	29		" 11 " " ARRAS	
	30		" 11 AM to Dugouts in NOMANS LAND St LAURENCE BLANGY.	
St LAURENT BLANGY.			Making new Trenches East of FAMPOUX in rear of front line - A B & C Companies north of Railway line - D Company S of Railway opposite CHEMICAL WORKS - The whole Battalion employed - Casualties 1 man killed 10 men wounded	

R.H.M. Clarke
LIEUT COLONEL
COMDG. 21ST S (PIONEER) Bn. WEST YORKS. REGT.

WAR DIARY or INTELLIGENCE SUMMARY

Army Form C. 2118.

21 W York Rg

Place	Date	Hour	Summary of Events and Information	Remarks and references to Appendices
ST LAURENT BLANGY	1917 May	1	Infantry strength Officers 36 Other Ranks 884. Continued the same work as last night, all Companies not Resting in Shelters.	
		2		
		3	Attack by 4th Division at 4.30 AM on ROEUX & CHEMICAL WORKS. A and 1/2 D Companies in readiness near 10th Brigade H.Q. as were Enemy ½ D Coy reply on line with 20th Lowlands - And the ½ D Coy Enemy reply on line of Enemy sent in the evening but the two Companies were employed in moving into line deepened - Casualties Captain J.P. MACKAY 2nd Lieut to communicating trench - C Coy carried water to 10th Brigade. Sergt KIMBERLEY, CARTER and CLAPHAM and 6 men wounded.	Casualties Killed - 6 wounded
		4	Camp shelled - Pte SUTCLIFFE killed - Sergt Major McLEAN and three men wounded - At night Companies working in and trenches and deepening them.	
		5	B C and D Companies working in front trenches - D Coy was heavily shelled with sprays. Total Casualties = Lieut PADGETT and Corporal NAIRN and 5 men killed; 20 men wounded.	

WAR DIARY
INTELLIGENCE SUMMARY
(Erase heading not required.)

Army Form C. 2118.

Place	Date	Hour	Summary of Events and Information	Remarks and references to Appendices
ST LAURENT BLANGY	May 1917	6	A, B and C Companies working in front trenches - a quiet night with no casualties -	
		7	A, C and D Companies working in front trenches - Casualties: 2 men killed and 5 wounded.	
		8	A, B and D Companies working in front trenches - Casualties: one man wounded -	
		9	B, D and C Companies working in front trenches	
		10	All Companies working in front trenches on final preparations - Casualties 4 men wounded.	
		11	A and B Companies rendezvous on North side of Railway Embankment South of FAMPOUX at 9 p.m. Following successful attack by the Division cut communication trenches South of the ARRAS–DOUAI Railway to ROEUX CHEMICAL WORKS and CEMETERY. Casualties 4 killed 13 wounded.	

WAR DIARY
or
INTELLIGENCE SUMMARY

(Erase heading not required.)

Army Form C. 2118.

Place	Date	Hour	Summary of Events and Information	Remarks and references to Appendices
ST LAURENT BLANGY	1917. May 12		A Company continuing new COLON trench Eastwards -	
		7	" " to construct Strong Points under 406th Field Coy R.E. but was not employed.	
		C	" " Making Strong Points near COLON trench with 9th Res.Coy	
			Casualties 8 men wounded.	
		13	General Lambton, Cmd.g IV Division, inspected the Battalion in Camp, and expressed his satisfaction with its work during these operations. The Division came out of the line and went back for rest -	
		14	Took up work on Reserve trench BLANGY under XVII Corps and worked for 15 until the end of the month, having no casualties.	
		31	Strength 17 Offrs, Others 35. O.R. 800.	

J.W.W Clarke Lt Col
Cmd.g M.f (Princess) West Yorkshire Regiment

WAR DIARY or INTELLIGENCE SUMMARY

Army Form C. 2118.

2/1 W York Rgt

(Erase heading not required.)

Instructions regarding War Diaries and Intelligence Summaries are contained in F.S. Regs., Part II. and the Staff Manual respectively. Title Pages will be prepared in manuscript.

Place	Date	Hour	Summary of Events and Information	Remarks and references to Appendices
ST LAURENT BLANGY	1917 June 11		Fighting Strength Officers 35 OR 800. Working on roads near BLANGY for XVII Corps until 15 & 12th inst with no casualties	
TRIANGLE	June 12		Mtn took march camp to the Triangle, ARRAS - DOUAI Railway south of the SCARPE - Built Shelters and other accommodation	
	June 13		Took up work for C.R.E, IV Division. A Coy making braid strong points in LANCER LANE. B Coy making Southern Communication Trench from LANCER LANE to BAYONET Trench. C Coy making Northern Communication Trench from CURRAH to CAMBRIAN & CUPID Support. D Coy deepening and widening Centre Communication Trench, CEYLON, from CRUMPS COROMA.	
	14		All work as usual - no casualties.	
	15		General Lambton visited new Camp. Work as usual. Casualties B Coy: 2 men wounded. C Coy: 4 men killed, 2 wounded.	
			do	

WAR DIARY or INTELLIGENCE SUMMARY

Army Form C. 2118.

Place	Date	Hour	Summary of Events and Information	Remarks and references to Appendices
TRIANGLE	June 16		Work as before. No Casualties; 1 man D Coy wounded	
	17		Work as before. D Coy also employed on Camouflage for Footpath along Railway Embankment from level Crossing on FAMPOUX – PELVES Road to Railway Bridge over Road from FAMPOUX to ROEUX. Casualties; 1 m.o., C Coy, Killed. 1 m.o., C Coy, Killed. (Works above) Casualties; 2 men wounded.	
	18		do. C Coy relieved in account of Brigade Relief. No Casualties.	
	19		do. C Coy joined B on Southern Communication Trench	
	20		do. Casualties: C Coy; 5 men killed, 7 wounded.	
	21		do. 1 man wounded	
	22		do.	
	23		All Companies got a night out in consequence of a Special permission by the 11th Brigade South of the SCARPE. Casualty, 1 man wounded	
	24		Church Parade at which the Rev. E. R. REID, C.F., attached to the Battalion since July 1915, preached his farewell sermon before returning to England. Work resumed by all Companies at night.	

Army Form C. 2118.

WAR DIARY
or
INTELLIGENCE SUMMARY
(Erase heading not required.)

Place	Date	Hour	Summary of Events and Information	Remarks and references to Appendices
TRIANGLE	1917 June 25		Work as before. C Coy working on LONE LANE. Carried 51 men wounded. General Lambton visited the Camp. Major BAMFORD went to Hospital with fever.	
	26		Work as before	
	27		do	
	28		do	
	29		do. D Company began new trench from CORDITE to CUSP near MOUNT PLEASANT Wood.	
	30		do.	
			Fighting Strength: Officers 32. O.R. 748	

J.W.W. Clarke. Lt.Col.
Comd. 21st (Pioneer) West Yorkshire Regiment

Army Form C. 2118.

WAR DIARY
or
INTELLIGENCE SUMMARY
21 W Yorks
(Erase heading not required.)

JM/14

Place	Date	Hour	Summary of Events and Information	Remarks and references to Appendices
TRIANGLE	July 1917		Fighting Strengths: Officers 32. O.R. 748 All companies working in Communication trenches & up to Support line – A Coy: Miners dugouts B Coy: Johnson Lane Communication trench C Coy: Lone Lane do D Coy: Cortile, Ceylon and rest trenches to CUSP. Casualty: 1 man A Coy wounded.	
	2		A Coy commenced new Dugout Coy H.Q. in WELLFORD TRENCH. Enemy shelled the trench severely and the 4 miners in southern Shaft were buried by a shell. 3 being killed – Sergt BROWNRIDGE. Another the survivor and a man of 2/4 Lancashire Fusiliers. Casualties: 3 killed, as above. 2 wounded	
	3		B, C & D Companies same work as before. Work as above. Casualties: 3 wounded. The Chaplain, the Rev. S. REID left the Battalion on completion of his year of service.	

2449 Wt. W14957/M90 750,000 1/16 J.B.C. & A. Forms/C.2118/12.

WAR DIARY
or
INTELLIGENCE SUMMARY

(Erase heading not required.)

Army Form C. 2118.

Place	Date	Hour	Summary of Events and Information	Remarks and references to Appendices
TRIANGLE	July 1917	4	Work as before – No casualties.	
		5	do	
		6	do	
		7	do Casualties: Sgt BOOTH slightly wounded – Casualties: Sgt HALL and 2 men, A Coy, wounded by shell on march up to trench – Pte OLDFIELD died of wounds later.	
		8	do No casualties.	
		9	do	
		10	do General LAMBTON visited Camp. No casualties. General LAMBTON presented Military Medals to Sergt BROWNRIDGE for gallantry rescuing 2 men buried by shell on 2nd inst: and to L/Cpl REYNOLDS and Pte MORGUE for rescuing a Gunner buried in an old shaft near MAUREPAS in 24th January –	
		11	Work as above. No casualties.	

WAR DIARY
or
INTELLIGENCE SUMMARY
(Erase heading not required.)

Army Form C. 2118.

Instructions regarding War Diaries and Intelligence Summaries are contained in F.S. Regs., Part II. and the Staff Manual respectively. Title Pages will be prepared in manuscript.

Place	Date	Hour	Summary of Events and Information	Remarks and references to Appendices
TRIANGLE	1917 July 12		Work as before. Casualties Sgt Davies, C Co, slightly wounded and two men A Coy bruised by shell, "Shell shock"	
	13		Work as before, except that A Company had 2 Platoons deepening and widening "MUSKET" trench. Casualty: 1 man wounded.	
	14		Work as above	
	15		do. B Company also improving LANCER LANE.	
	16		do	
	17		do	
	18		do	
	19		do. Casualty: 1 man, C Coy, wounded.	
	20		do	
	21		do. C Coy commenced new Fire trench from MUSKET trench to ORANGE STREET. Casualties Sgt HODGSON and 3 men of C Coy and one man of A Coy wounded.	

WAR DIARY or INTELLIGENCE SUMMARY.

Army Form C. 2118.

Place	Date 1917	Hour	Summary of Events and Information	Remarks and references to Appendices
TRIANGLE	July 22		Work as before Casualty one man of "B" Coy wounded	
"	" 23		" " " " Casualties four men of "A" Coy killed by 2nd Lt MacDougall & one man "A" Coy wounded } shell "C" Coy at rest three men of "C" Coy wounded } fire	
"	" 24		Both as above except) Casualties "D" Coy start work on CORONA-CUSP switch	
"	" 25		With as above except "B" Coy improve LANCER LANE	
"	" 26		do do "	
"	" 27		do do " 2nd Lt W.R. RICHARDSON reported	
"	" 28		do do and one Platoon of "C" Coy work on CURB LANE	
"	" 29		"A", "C" & "D" Coy work as before "B" Coy at rest & training	
"	" 30		do do do	
"	" 31		do do do	
			Strength on 31-7-17 30 officers 751 O.R.	

E. Yenn. Major
LIEUT. COLONEL
COMDG. 21ST (PIONEER) Bn. WEST YORKS REGT.

INTELLIGENCE SUMMARY

21st (Reserve) Battalion
West Riding

Summary of Events and Information

Place	Date	Hour	
	29 July		Strength 30 Officers, 732 OR
		2	A Coy & B Coy on regimental duties – B Coy at training in camp
		3	do
		4	do
		5	B Coy to trench to attack in Rainbow wood. C Coy came to training in camp. Companies went on fatigues as follows — A Coy in MUSKET B Coy OLR B SMELT and machine gun School. C Coy to fatigue the GENTRE. D Coy on GENTRE all day extended order drill, bomb & Lewis Gun Coarse. Cable Wire 3 men. B Company Nominated.
		6	Holt no stores — B Company employed Rifle Corps with R.F.C. Transport to collect for a bath for inspecting the troops marching past with no stores.
		7	1 Man A Coy sent Boy Instructional School to inspection only to tea?
		8	Holt no stores do
		9	do
		10	do

WAR DIARY
INTELLIGENCE SUMMARY

(Erase heading not required.)

Date	Hour	Summary of Events and Information	Remarks and references to Appendices

INTELLIGENCE SUMMARY

(Erasures not permitted.)

Summary of Events and Information

Place	Date	Hour	
FRANCE	Jul 22		Wakefield
	23		do
	24		do
	25		do
	26		B Coy. set to trenches & M.A. duties. Missed out camps
			A Coy. Left for Ridoubt on R. West Rd. Reserve.
			C Coy. entrained for CURIS-SULTET
			D Coy. entrained for DICKEMM and thereafter S.P. at SCHERPE
	27		Work as above
	28		do
	29		do
	30		do
	31		do
			Eighteenth a/c. Miars

O.R.B.
M.W. Parker Lt Col
Commanding 9th Royal Northumberland Fusiliers

WAR DIARY or INTELLIGENCE SUMMARY.

(Erase heading not required.)

Army Form C. 2118.

21 W York R

9/16

Place	Date	Hour	Summary of Events and Information	Remarks and references to Appendices
TRIANGLE	1917 Sept 1		A Company reconstructing WELFORD Reserve	
			B " erecting NISSEN Hut Camps	
			C " reconstructing CURB Switch and maintaining all Communication Trenches South of the SCARPE.	
			D " working on CORONA Switch and CORDITE Reserve and maintaining all Communication Trenches north of the SCARPE.	
	2		Work as above.	
	3		do	
	4		do	
	5		do	
	6		do	
	7		Handed over all work to Pioneer Battn - GORDON Highlanders, XV Division.	
	8		Battalion marched to Camp at BLAIRVILLE for rest and training, having been at work continuously since 30th April.	
BLAIRVILLE	9th to 15th		Battalion remained at BLAIRVILLE for rest and training and who inspected during 15 period by Major Gnl LAMBTON cmdg 2nd Division and Gnl HALDANE cmdg VI Corps.	

Army Form C. 2118.

WAR DIARY
or
INTELLIGENCE SUMMARY.
(Erase heading not required.)

Instructions regarding War Diaries and Intelligence Summaries are contained in F.S. Regs, Part II. and the Staff Manual respectively. Title pages will be prepared in manuscript.

Place	Date	Hour	Summary of Events and Information	Remarks and references to Appendices
	1917			
BLAIRVILLE	Sept 20		Battalion moved by rail to PESELHOEK and thence marched to Camp "PHEASANT" near PROVEN.	
PHEASANT Camp, PROVEN.	21 22 23 24		Rest and Training	
	25		C Company proceeded to CANAL BANK by BARD COTTAGE for work with 20th Division. A, B and D Companies continued training.	
	26		Lewis gun detachment prepared for relief of Pioneer Bn of 20th Div.	
	27		Lewis gun detachment proceeded to CANAL BANK. One man C Coy wounded.	
	28		B, C and D Companies with Head Quarters moved to Canal Bank	
YSER CANAL BANK	29		Relieving 11th Bn (Pioneers) Durham L.I. A Company proceeded to St SIXTE for work on Railways under A.D.L.R. C Company rejoined H.Qrs. Work of Northern Pioneers continued. One man C Coy wounded. B Coy making Tramways and Road formations on STEENBEEK. C Coy erecting and maintaining Tramways	

T2131. Wt. W708—776. 500000. 4/15. Sir J.C. & S.

Army Form C. 2118.

WAR DIARY
or
INTELLIGENCE SUMMARY.
(Erase heading not required.)

Instructions regarding War Diaries and Intelligence Summaries are contained in F.S. Regs., Part II. and the Staff Manual respectively. Title pages will be prepared in manuscript.

Place	Date	Hour	Summary of Events and Information	Remarks and references to Appendices
YSER CANAL BANK	Sept 29		1917	
			B Coy: ½ Coy trekking with B and ½ Coy with C.	
	30		Work as yesterday - 4 men of C Coy killed - Fighting Strength Officers 29. O.R. 756 -	
			J.M. [signature] Lieut. Col.	
			Comdg 2/1st (S) (Princess) West Yorkshire Regiment.	

Army Form C. 2118.

21 W York 251
P/4

WAR DIARY
or
INTELLIGENCE SUMMARY.
(Erase heading not required.)

Instructions regarding War Diaries and Intelligence Summaries are contained in F. S. Regs., Part II. and the Staff Manual respectively. Title pages will be prepared in manuscript.

Place	Date	Hour	Summary of Events and Information	Remarks and references to Appendices
YSER CANAL BANK	1917 Oct	1st	"A" Company on railway, A Line ST SIXTE; B,C,D Coys extending tramways STEENBEEK to LANGEMARCK	Casualties nil.
	"	2nd	A + C Coys work as yesterday, B + D erecting camouflage screens at MARSOUIN FARM and GAITY FARM, laying 1st dry-weather track & footing it.	9 wounded
	"	3rd	Work as yesterday	Casualties nil.
	"	4th	B, C + D repairing roads & tramways. deck board track SANDY FM TO IRIS	1 killed, 7 wounded
	"	4th	Division attached inst. M.G. POELCAPPELLE	8 wounded with the division.
	"	4th	"A" Coy attached 27th YORKS & LANCS. and camped at B.23.d.98 Sheet 28	
	"	5th	Work a. above. A Coy on light railway construction at RUDOLPH FARM.	2 wounded
	"	6th	B + D Coys on road ALOUETTE FM to LANGEMARCK "C" on tramways, "A" as above	3 "
	"	7th	Work a. above	1 "
	"	8th	do do	13 "
	"	9th	IV Division attached again. B, C + D Coys repaired SCHREIBOOM - POELCAPPELLE Road up to V.19.a.72. A on railway at RUDOLPH FARM.	1 killed, 15 wounded
	"	10th	Work as above. Lt.Col.Sir.E.H.St.L. Clarke Bart, D.S.O. wounded in leg. Work on road done by daylight	3 killed
	"	11th	do do	3 wounded

T2134. Wt. W708-776. 500000. 4/15. Sir J. C. & S.

Army Form C. 2118.

WAR DIARY
or
INTELLIGENCE SUMMARY.
(Erase heading not required.)

Instructions regarding War Diaries and Intelligence Summaries are contained in F. S. Regs., Part II. and the Staff Manual respectively. Title pages will be prepared in manuscript.

Place	Date	Hour	Summary of Events and Information	Remarks and references to Appendices
YSER CANAL BANK.	Oct.	12th	"B, C & D" Coys draining road PILCKEM – POELCAPPELLE. "A" Coy on light railway. 1 killed 6 wounded	Casualties nil.
	"	13th	Work as above	1 wounded.
	"	14th	do	
	"	15th	do	Casualties nil.
	"	16th	Battalion less A Coy moved to SARAWAK CAMP S1. Area. IV DIVISION. Coy Artillery & Pioneers move to 3rd Army Area.	
	"	17th	Rest & cleaning up	
	"	18th	do do	
	"	19th	Battalion marched to B11 d33 Sheet 28 & pitched camp. Transport to B14 a55.	
	"	20th	Battalion at work on light railways under A2LR5 WARWICK to HANLEY SWITCH. 5 wounded.	
CHASSEUR FARM	"	21st	Work as above BIRMINGHAM to VULCAN line.	5 "
	"	22nd	do do Lt HANSON wounded.	7 O.R. "
	"	23rd	"A" Coy rejoin Battalion 4 Coys work as above	2 "
	"	24th	do do	Casualties nil.
	"	25th	do do	1 wounded.
	"	26th	"A" Coy at work with 7th YORK & LANCS. B, C & D work as above	Casualties nil.

T2134. Wt. W708–776. 500000. 4/15. Sir J. C. & S.

Army Form C. 2118.

WAR DIARY
or
INTELLIGENCE SUMMARY.
(Erase heading not required.)

Place	Date	Hour	Summary of Events and Information	Remarks and references to Appendices
CHASSEUR FARM B.11.d.33	Oct. 27th		"A" Coy work at PHEASANT FM. B.C & D on BIRMINGHAM — LANGEMARCK line attended A.D.L.R.S. 7 wounded	
"	" 28th		do. Casualties nil	
"	" 29th		do. 3 wounded	
"	" 30th		do. Casualties nil	
"	" 31st		do. 2 killed 2 wounded	
			Heavy bombing at night by enemy on 30th & 31st Fighting Strength 28 officers 696 O.R.	
			Edwin Finn Major for Lt Col commanding 21st Bn (Pioneers) West Yorkshire Regt.	

Instructions regarding War Diaries and Intelligence Summaries are contained in F.S. Regs., Part II. and the Staff Manual respectively. Title pages will be prepared in manuscript.

Army Form C. 2118.

WAR DIARY
or
INTELLIGENCE SUMMARY.
(Erase heading not required.)

Place	Date	Hour	Summary of Events and Information	Remarks and references to Appendices
CHASSEUR FARM, BOESINGHE	1917 Nov	1st	Fighting Strength 28 Officers 696 O.R. Battalion constructing light railway from BIRMINGHAM to LANGEMARCK under A.D.L.R.5	
	"	2nd	2 men killed 1 wounded by bomb dropped by the enemy on a dug-out on night 31st/1st. Strength eff. expecting orders to move to 3rd Army area. I attended on 1st Nov.	
	"	3rd	do	
	"	4th	do	
	"	5th	Personnel of Batt. moved by bus to ESTAIRES, transport by road.	
	"	6th	Battalion marched to BETHUNE	
	"	7th	" " to PETIT SERVINS	
	"	8th	" " to ARRAS	
ARRAS	"	9th	"A" Coy worked on tramway on CAMBRAI ROAD. Men had baths + rested.	
	"	10th	"B" Coy build NISSEN HUTS in RONVILLE. Draft of 289 O.R. to R.E. joined	
	"	11th	Draft of 289 O.R. sent to reinforce infantry battalions of WEST YORKS. REGT.	
TILLOY	"	12th	Battalion marched into camp in TILLOY WOOD.	
	"	13th	Upkeep of communication trenches and tramway, 1 platoon on NISSEN hut building. do	

WAR DIARY or INTELLIGENCE SUMMARY

Army Form C. 2118.

Place	Date	Hour	Summary of Events and Information	Remarks and references to Appendices
TILLOY	1917 Nov 14th		Work on communication trenches & tramway; 1 platoon on NISSEN hut building	20 O.R. transferred to infantry.
"	" 15th		do	Casualties 2 men wounded.
"	" 16th		do	" nil
"	" 17th		do	" O.R. 2 wounded.
"	" 18th		do	" nil
"	" 19th		do putting in artillery bridges	" nil. 45 O.R. transferred to R.E.
"	" 20th		do	" O.R. 3 wounded.
"	" 21st		do	" nil
"	" 22nd		do	" nil
"	" 23rd		do	" O.R. 4 wounded
"	" 24th		do	" nil
"	" 25th		do	" nil
"	" 26th		do	" nil
"	" 27th		do ½ Batt resting	" 1 O.R. wounded.
"	" 28th		do ½ Batt resting	" 1 O.R. wounded
"	" 29th		do	" 1 killed 1 wounded

Army Form C. 2118.

WAR DIARY
or
INTELLIGENCE SUMMARY.
(Erase heading not required.)

Instructions regarding War Diaries and Intelligence Summaries are contained in F. S. Regs., Part II. and the Staff Manual respectively. Title pages will be prepared in manuscript.

Place	Date	Hour	Summary of Events and Information	Remarks and references to Appendices
TILLOY	1917. Nov 30th		Work on communication trenches, tramway & machine gun post  1 O.R. wounded 2 O.R. gassed. Fighting Strength 34 officers 717 O.R. Edwin Fenn Lt Col. Commanding 21st/13th West Yorkshire Regt (Pioneers).	

WAR DIARY

INTELLIGENCE SUMMARY
(Erase heading not required.)

Army Form C. 2118.

21 W[...]

Place	Date	Hour	Summary of Events and Information	Remarks and references to Appendices
TILLOY	1917. Dec 1st		Fighting strength 34 Officers 717 other ranks. A, B + D Coys. Maintenance of communication trenches. C Coy constructing trench tramway	Casualties nil.
"	2nd		do	" 2 O.R. wounded
"	3rd		do	" nil.
"	4th		do	" nil.
"	5th		Work as above + ½ Coy "C" wiring Reserve Line	" nil
"	6th		do	" 1 O.R. wounded
"	7th		do	" nil
"	8th		do	" 1 O.R. wounded
"	9th		do	" nil
"	10th		do. Battalion ordered to stand-to each morning	
"	11th		do. "A" Company shelled on CAMBRAI ROAD 2 killed 5 wounded	
"	12th		do.	Casualties nil
"	13th		do. 50 O.R. sent to R.E. Base Depot, ROUEN	1 O.R. wounded.

Army Form C. 2118.

WAR DIARY
INTELLIGENCE SUMMARY.
(Erase heading not required.)

Instructions regarding War Diaries and Intelligence Summaries are contained in F.S. Regs., Part II. and the Staff Manual respectively. Title pages will be prepared in manuscript.

Place	Date	Hour	Summary of Events and Information	Remarks and references to Appendices
TILLOY	Dec 14th		Inantenance of trenches + wiring reserve line + TWIN COPSES Casualties	nil
"	" 15th		do	nil
"	" 16th		2nd ESSEX raid LONG TRENCH at 13hrs working parties withdrawn "	"
"	" 17th		Both as above "	2 O.R. wounded
"	" 18th		do "	nil
"	" 19th		do Battalion cease to stand to at dawn "	nil
"	" 20th		do "	nil
"	" 21st		do Reinforcement 32 O.R. "	nil
"	" 22nd		do "	nil
"	" 23rd		do Reinforcement 6 O.R. "	2 O.R. killed
"	" 24th		do "	Casualties nil
"	" 25th		do Small parties maintain trenches; remainder, no work "	nil
"	" 26th		do "	nil
"	" 27th		do Fire-steps formed in communication trenches as part of defence scheme "	nil
			Reinforcement 13 O.R.	

Army Form C. 2118.

WAR DIARY
INTELLIGENCE SUMMARY.
(Erase heading not required.)

Place	Date	Hour	Summary of Events and Information	Remarks and references to Appendices
TILLOY	1917			
	Dec 28th		Maintenance of trenches, digging pre-steps in communication trenches as part of defence scheme. Casualties nil.	
"	" 29th		do do + strong points do nil	
"	" 30th		do do do do nil	
"	" 31st		do do do do	
			100 O.R. sent to 1/5th & 15th W. YORKSHIRE REGT. Reinforcement 97 O.R. of Class B, men. Casualties 10 O.R. killed 30 O.R. wounded.	
			2 teams of Lewis gunners employed on anti-aircraft work during the month. Fighting strength 33 officers 697 O.R.	

Edwin Finn Lt Col
Commanding 21st Bn (Pioneers) West Yorkshire Regt.

Army Form C. 2118.

WAR DIARY
INTELLIGENCE SUMMARY.
(Erase heading not required.)

Instructions regarding War Diaries and Intelligence Summaries are contained in F. S. Regs., Part II. and the Staff Manual respectively. Title pages will be prepared in manuscript.

Northern Yorks Regiment Vol 20

Place	Date	Hour	Summary of Events and Information	Remarks and references to Appendices
TILLOY	1918 Jan 1st		Fighting Strength 34 officers 599 O.R.	
	" 2nd		"A" Company being in dug-outs at HAPPY VALLEY H36a11 Sheet 51B N.W. 1/20,000 Maintenance of communication trenches & prestyping dams, digging strongpoints and maintaining tramways.	
	" 3rd		both as above	Casualties nil.
	" 4th		do + machine gun nest begun in HAPPY VALLEY	" nil.
	" 5th		do do continued	" nil.
	" 6th		do do	" nil.
	" 7th		do do	1 O.R. killed
	" 8th		do do	Casualties nil
	" 9th		do do	" nil.
	" 10th		do do	" nil.
	" 11th		"B" Company revetting CIRCLE TRENCH A, C, + D Coys. as above	" nil.
	" 12th		do do	" nil.
	" 13th		do do m/gun nest I'vo begun	" nil.

Army Form C. 2118.

T2134. Wt. W708—776. 5000000. 4/15. Sir J. C. & S.

WAR DIARY
INTELLIGENCE SUMMARY.
(Erase heading not required.)

Army Form C. 2118.

Place	Date	Hour	Summary of Events and Information	Remarks and references to Appendices
TILLOY	1918			
	Jan. 14th		Maintenance of Communication trenches & tramway; construction of strong points & reform rest at HAPPY VALLEY. 7 Officers from the Battalion	Casualties nil.
"	15th		do work as above	" nil.
"	16th		A Coy relieving B.C & D Coys start work on Support Line & 2nd system of trenches.	" nil.
"	17th		All Coys work on new Support Line & 2nd system behind FORK & CURB trenches	" nil.
"	18th		Rain after frost caused collapse of trenches on 17th & 18th; digging new trenches abandoned. Communication trenches impassable. Duckboard which board tracks have been laid.	
			A + B Coys reclaim SPADE RESERVE. C + D Coys revet new Support ahead dug.	Casualties nil.
"	19th		do do	" nil.
"	20th		do do	" nil.
"	21st		do do	" nil.
"	22nd		do do	2 O.R wounded.
"	23rd		"C+D" as above + reclaiming WELLFORD + CURB trenches	
"	24th		All companies revetting Reserve Line + small parties on new Support line behind Reserve line	Casualties nil.
"	25th		do as above	" nil.

Army Form C. 2118.

WAR DIARY
INTELLIGENCE SUMMARY.
(Erase heading not required.)

Instructions regarding War Diaries and Intelligence Summaries are contained in F. S. Regs., Part II. and the Staff Manual respectively. Title pages will be prepared in manuscript.

Place	Date	Hour	Summary of Events and Information	Remarks and references to Appendices
TILLOY	1918			
	Jan 26th		All Coys reclaiming & revetting Reserve line & new Support line (2 Coys) casualties nil	
	" 27th		do	" nil.
	" 28th		do	" nil.
	" 29th		do	1 O.R. wounded.
	" 30th		do	" nil
	" 31st		Reinforcement 86 O.R.	
			Work as above	1 O.R. killed
			Fighting Strength 38 Officers 757 O.R.	

Edwin Lomm Lt Col.
Commanding 21st/15th (Pioneers) West Yorkshire Regiment.

WAR DIARY or INTELLIGENCE SUMMARY.

(Erase heading not required.)

Army Form C. 2118.

Place	Date	Hour	Summary of Events and Information	Remarks and references to Appendices
TILLOY	1918 Feb 1st		Fighting strength 37 Officers 757 O.R. Battn. reclaiming + revising reserve trenches, control of rear of transways	
"	" 2nd		do as above. G.O.C. inspected transport of battalion	
"	" 3rd		do	
"	" 4th		2 Officers + 40 O.R. from 15th Bn W.Y.R. join	
"	" 5th		50 O.R. ex R.E. shafted to ROUEN. 1 O.R. wounded	
"	" 6th		do ("D" Coy move to billets in ARRAS after relief by 9th GORDON HIGHLRS)	
"	" 7th		do	
ARRAS	" 8th		Remainder of Battalion moves to billets in ARRAS	
"	" 10th		Company training, football + tug-of-war	
"	" 12th		do do Advance parties go to St LAURENT BLANGY.	
"	" 13th		do do inspects billets.	
"	" 14th		do G.O.C. inspects billets.	
"	" 15th		G.O.C. inspects battalion in marching order. A, B + D Coys move to St LAURENT BLANGY + STIRLING CAMP M.Q. X SCARPE	
St LAURENT BLANGY	" 16th		"C" Coy move to LES FOSSES FARM for work under C.R.E. 15th Div. 1 O.R. wounded.	

T2134. Wt. W708—776. 500000. 4/15. Sir J. C. & S.

WAR DIARY
INTELLIGENCE SUMMARY
(Erase heading not required.)

Army Form C. 2118.

Instructions regarding War Diaries and Intelligence Summaries are contained in F. S. Regs., Part II. and the Staff Manual respectively. Title pages will be prepared in manuscript.

Place	Date	Hour	Summary of Events and Information	Remarks and references to Appendices
ST LAURENT BLANGY	1918 Feb. 17th		Battalion (less 1 Coy) digging + wiring reserve trench 3rd System on each side of R.SCARPE. "C" Coy wiring GORDON AVENUE. 5 O.R. wounded.	
"	" 18th		Not as above	
"	" 19th		do	
"	" 20th		do Casualties 1 Officer + 3 O.R. M.Y. gassed	
"	" 21st		do	
"	" 22nd		do + Started 2 deep dug-outs	
"	" 23rd		do	
"	" 24th		do	
"	" 25th		Casualties 3 O.R. wounded	
"	" 26th		G.O.C. inspected billets + transport. Battalion reorganized into three companies.	
"	" 28th		2/Lt Mitchell joined the battalion Fighting Strength 40 Officers 749 O.R.	

Comm'g 21st B'n (Pioneers) West Yorkshire Regt.
Edwin Finn Lt Col

Pioneers.
4th Div.

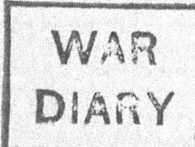

21st BATTN. THE WEST YORKSHIRE REGIMENT.

M A R C H

1 9 1 8

21 W

WAR DIARY
or
INTELLIGENCE SUMMARY
(Erase heading not required.)

Army Form C.-2118.

Instructions regarding War Diaries and Intelligence Summaries are contained in F.S. Regs., Part II. and the Staff Manual respectively. Title pages will be prepared in manuscript.

Place	Date	Hour	Summary of Events and Information	Remarks and references to Appendices
	1916			
S⁺ LAURENT BLANGY	March 1		Working Strength 15 March 40 Offrs 749 OR	
	2		Three Companies working on Reserve Trenches for XVII Corps, less ½ a Coy lent to XV Division	
	3 (Sunday)		do	
	4		do	
	5		do	
	6		do	
	7		do	2 men wounded
	8		do	
	9		do	
	10		do	
	11		½ Coy ceased duty with XV Division	50 O.R. joined
ARRAS	12		Battalion moved into Billets in ARRAS Resting	50 OR joined
	13		All four Companies working on Reserve Trenches for XVII Corps	
	14		do	

Army Form C. 2118.

INTELLIGENCE SUMMARY.
(Erase heading not required.)

Instructions regarding War Diaries and Intelligence Summaries are contained in F. S. Regs., Part II. and the Staff Manual respectively. Title pages will be prepared in manuscript.

Place	Date 1916	Hour	Summary of Events and Information	Remarks and references to Appendices
ARRAS	March 15		All three Companies employed in Reserve lines for Working Coys.	
	16		do	
	17		do 26 O.R. joined	
	18		do	
	19		do	
	20		do	
	21		do 1st M.O. E.CLARKE joined. 2 men wounded.	
	22		The Battalion marched to RIFLE CAMP. 1 man wounded	
RIFLE CAMP	23		At dawn sent one company to 2nd Brigade to occupy Reserve Trenches. Received orders in C.O. to move back to DUIZANS for work at my lines. Notified Companies and left camp at 10 P.M. - { Major FINN severely wounded. 4 men wounded.	
DUIZANS	24		Arrived DUIZANS 1 A.M. Worked on Army lines 9 a.m. to 5 p.m.	
	25		Continued the work. Received orders to march to RIFLE CAMP and arrived there at midnight. J.O.R. joined	
RIFLE CAMP	26		Sent Companies into the Reserve Trenches at dawn. Companies at work improving their Trenches.	

WAR DIARY or INTELLIGENCE SUMMARY

(Erase heading not required.)

Army Form C. 2118.

Place	Date	Hour	Summary of Events and Information	Remarks and references to Appendices
RIFLE CAMP	1918 Mch 27		Companies at work improving Rear Trenches — heavy casualties to X Coy by shell fire. 16 killed and 42 wounded.	
	28		Battalion attached to 10th Brigade, holding loving long line South of the SCARPE. At 6.30 PM moved forward in conjunction with 2 CR Duke of Wellingtons and a Battalion K.O.S.B. of the 15th Division and took up position about 1000 yards in front, dug in and held the position. Casualties 8 killed 40 wounded.	
	29		Improved trench and position. 12 ofnrs 1 OR gassed. Relieved by R. Warwicks during the night. 2 OR wounded.	
	30		Battalion reassembled in RIFLE CAMP at 4 AM and moved in the afternoon to Dugouts on St LAURENT BLANGY taking up work on the Inter -mediate line N of the ARRAS-FAMPOUX Road.	
St LAURENT BLANGY.	31		Work continued. R.S.M. GIBBS wounded. 10 R wounded. Fighting strength Offrs 25. OR 551.	

S.M. Ted Clarke Lt Colonel
Comdg. 21st West Yorkshire Regt.
(Pioneers)

4th Divisional Pioneers

21st BATTALION

WEST YORKSHIRE REGIMENT (Pioneers)

APRIL 1918.

WAR DIARY or INTELLIGENCE SUMMARY

Army Form C. 2118.

21 W York R (?) 23

Place	Date	Hour	Summary of Events and Information	Remarks and references to Appendices
ST AGREST BLANGY	1918 Aug 1		Fighting Strength Officers 25 – OR 551. Y Coy & worK under 12th Brigade and garrison EFFIE TRENCH X and Z Coy working in enemy intermediate Trench. Crawley (Tunnels)	
	2		Work as above	
	3		do	
	4		X Coy work intermediate line & 10th Bde Y " EFFIE TRENCH for 12th Bde Z " CASTLE LANE for 11th Bde	
	5		Work as above – Sergt RICHARDSON and 3 men X Coy wounded	
	6		Casualties X Coy 1 Killed (?), and 2 wounded. Lieutenant (?) pro shell burst in the entrance to the Micro' them. A Z Coy and 5 Officers were fatally gassed. Capt DIGHTON, Lieuts WICKLEBRIDGE, FOSTER, FOX, and Chaplain Rev C. WRIGHT. Also Pte WORMALDE.	
	7		The Battalion was relieved by the 1st Can. Division. Y Coy first at night & moved to from to SIMENCOURT. X and Z worked as before.	

T2131. Wt. W708—776. 500000. 4/15. Sir J. C. & S.

Army Form C. 2118.

WAR DIARY
or
INTELLIGENCE SUMMARY.
(Erase heading not required.)

Instructions regarding War Diaries and Intelligence Summaries are contained in F. S. Regs., Part II. and the Staff Manual respectively. Title pages will be prepared in manuscript.

Place	Date	Hour	Summary of Events and Information	Remarks and references to Appendices
FOSSEUX	1918	8	The X and Z Co with H.Q. moved by train to FOSSEUX in relief of 1st CANADIAN PIONEERS and settled down for rest and cleaning up in Huts.	
		9	A fresh draft of reinforcement arrived 10 officers, 199 O.R. Proceeded to baths just under 19	
		10	33 O.R. reinforcements came in.	
		11	Harvey returns to duties -	
		12	Battalion marched at 10.30 AM to SUN BURNING PRINT at the ARRAS-DOULLENS Road where it was kept waiting from 12 to 4 P.M. for busses - moved to a point between VILLERS and BUSNES and bivouacked in fields.	
LE CORNET BOURDOIS		13	Moved to billets in LE CORNET BOURDOIS. Arrived. Billets at the CHATEAU DE VERPPE.	
		14	All companies working at night on trenches at LES HARISOIRS on a track following the road which is the line of the Enemy Barrage. X Coy had 2/Lieut PLUMER and 10 men wounded.	

T2134. Wt. W708—776. 500000. 4/15. Sir J. C. & S.

WAR DIARY or INTELLIGENCE SUMMARY

(Erase heading not required.)

Army Form C. 2118.

Instructions regarding War Diaries and Intelligence Summaries are contained in F.S. Regs., Part II. and the Staff Manual respectively. Title pages will be prepared in manuscript.

Place	Date	Hour	Summary of Events and Information	Remarks and references to Appendices
CHATEAU de WERPPE	1916 Apl 15		Work as yesterday - Strgth R.17 O.R arrived -	
		16	do Casualties; 1 man Y Co wounded. Transport moved from LE CORNET BOURDOIS to BUSCHETTES.	
		17	Three Companies digging new trenches between HINGES and the CANAL. Cas: 1 man wounded	
		18	X and Y as yesterday - Z Coy new trench near LES HARISOIRS. Casualties: Lt METCALFE SMITH wounded (died of wounds) 4 men wounded	
		#	Y Company 3 men killed and 9 wounded from MG shell on the way to work. On this day a strong enemy attack on 4th Division front was completed beaten off and about 160 Prisoners were taken.	
		19	X continued same work - Y trenches East of HINGES. Z Trenches LES HARISOIRS. Casualties: 6 men wounded.	
		20	X Coy one Platoon North East of Canal - The other 3 Platoons were shelled off and worked on previous work East of LA KLOUY FARM - Lieut J B GRANGE was killed. 2 men killed and 8 men wounded - Y Coy making new lines at Mont BERNENCHON - Z Coy LES HARISOIRS	
		21	2/Lt J. CAMPLIN and 2/Lt G. H. PRIDMORE transferred to 2nd ESSEX Regt which was short of Officers. Lieut GRANGE's kit also volunteered for transfer but was killed last night.	

T.2134. Wt. W708—776. 500000. 4/15. Sir J. C. & S.

Army Form C. 2118.

WAR DIARY
or
INTELLIGENCE SUMMARY
(Erase heading not required.)

Instructions regarding War Diaries and Intelligence Summaries are contained in F. S. Regs., Part II. and the Staff Manual respectively. Title pages will be prepared in manuscript.

Place	Date	Hour	Summary of Events and Information	Remarks and references to Appendices
CHATEAU de WERPPE.	1918. Apl 21		Companies at same work as yesterday – Cas. 1 man wounded.	
	22		do Cas. 3 men wounded.	
	23		do Cas. 1 man wounded.	
	24		Draft of 37 O.R. arrived – X Coy on trench N of LA PLOUY FARM. Y Coy continuing this line to HINGES. Z Coy continuing line through HINGES – This Company was heavily shelled and had casualties. Cpl HAINSWORTH and 5 men wounded and 8 men gassed. Work as yesterday. Casualties. Sgt TAYLOR and 2 men wounded.	
	25			
	26		X Coy on trench behind front line at RIEZ-DU-VINAGE. Y and Z as yesterday. At the work 1 man was wounded – In Camp at about 9.P.M. the enemy shelled the huts heavily for five minutes – fortunately the working parties were all out – The Casualties were 5 men killed; 27 men wounded; and 14 men gassed.	
	27		X and Y off work. Z Coy working in PACAUT WOOD N of CANAL. Arranged the Companies in Battalions to march Camp so far as possible – Y Company dug in on West bank of CLARENCE River.	

T.1134. Wt. W708-776. 500000. 4/15. Sir J. C. & S.

Army Form C. 2118.

WAR DIARY
or
INTELLIGENCE SUMMARY.
(Erase heading not required.)

Instructions regarding War Diaries and Intelligence Summaries are contained in F. S. Regs., Part II. and the Staff Manual respectively. Title pages will be prepared in manuscript.

Place	Date	Hour	Summary of Events and Information	Remarks and references to Appendices
CHATEAU de WERPPE	1918. April	28	2/Lt A. RACE joined. Moved Z Coy to Farm at LENGLET and started Nissen huts there & Nissen huts for the Company.	
		28	X Coy at work in PACAUT WOOD. Y Coy Wiring at RIEZ-DU-VINAGE. Z Coy at work in PACAUT WOOD. Casualties 6 wounded	
		29	Started X Coy to Nissen huts and cottages by Z Coy Farm — Companies worked as yesterday. Casualties 3 wounded —	
		30	Head Quarters and Y Company moved from the Chateau to Farms in LA VALLÉE, erecting Nissen huts in the Orchards. X and Z Companies worked as yesterday. Y Coy Wiring from near BAQUEROLLES Farm to RIEZ-DU-VINAGE.	
			Strength May 28 Officers and 533 O.R.	

E.M.H. Clarke Lt Col.
Com.d 21st (S) West Yorkshire Regiment
(PIONEERS)

T2134. Wt. W708—776. 500000. 4/15. Sir J. C. & S.

WAR DIARY
or
INTELLIGENCE SUMMARY.
(Erase heading not required.)

Army Form C. 2118.

Place	Date	Hour	Summary of Events and Information	Remarks and references to Appendices
LA VALLÉE	1918 May 1		Strength: 28 Officers 633 O.R. X Coy cleaning in PACAUT WOOD and making road near LECAUROY. Y Coy improving Reserve line of front system. Z Coy building Breastworks and Posts in PACAUT WOOD. Casualties 1 man wounded.	M¹ Westergate M. Fyfe
	2		X and Y Companies employed on Reserve line of front System which is to be trench bonded and revetted. Z on front, to dig shelters to be splinter proof shelters for garrison. Casualty 1 man wounded.	
	3		Z Coy as yesterday. Work as yesterday.	
	4		do Casualty 1 man wounded.	
	5		X and Y did not work owing to thunderstorm at night	
	6		Z Coy day work as yesterday Work as before	
	7		X Coy Training Support line - Interfered with by shelling. Y " Reserve line - Z Coy work as yesterday. Casualties Y Coy, 1 killed 9 wounded.	

WAR DIARY or INTELLIGENCE SUMMARY

Army Form C. 2118.

Place	Date	Hour	Summary of Events and Information	Remarks and references to Appendices
LA VALLÉE	1918 May 8		X & Y Companies erecting Wire in Canal Bank	
			Z Coy work as yesterday in PACAUT WOOD. Cas: 1 man wounded	
		9	do	
			X and Y Coy did not work at night. the Battalion being held in readiness for defence of CLARENCE RIVER switch in case of attack which was expected but did not come off. No casualties	
		10	X Coy erected 1000 yards of wire in front of 1st line of 2nd system – day	
			Y Coy wiring Canal Bank – Z Coy wiring French —	
		11	X Coy digging trench, support line, second system	
			Y and Z Companies do to yesterday —	
		12	X Coy wiring in front of support line 1st system	
			Y do	
			2 days work on trench as yesterday – Night wiring support line, much	
			interfered with by shell fire. Cas: 3 men wounded.	
		13	X & Y Companies deepening revetting and broadening Reserve Line	
			Z Coy improving Front line 2nd System at LES HARISOIRS	
			Casualties. Y Coy – 1 killed 3 wounded	

Army Form C. 2118.

WAR DIARY
or
INTELLIGENCE SUMMARY.
(Erase heading not required.)

Place	Date	Hour	Summary of Events and Information	Remarks and references to Appendices
La VALLÉE	1918 May 14		Work as yesterday -	
	15		do	
	16		do	Cas: 2 wounded
	17		do	Cas: 6 wounded (2 died of wounds)
	18		do	2 Coy also wiring from PACAUTWOOD
	19		do	do
	20		do	Casualties: 2 killed 2 wounded
	21		do	All companies wiring also at night
	22		do	do
	23		do	Cas: 1 man wounded.
	24		do	
	25		do	
	26		X and Y Companies finished switch line & wire on 1250 yd Ay	
			and carrying all materials - Z Coy do yesterday -	
				Casualties: 6 men gas -
	27		X Coy completed wiring and started a alternative trench - Z do yesterday	

T2134. Wt. W708—776. 500000. 4/15. Sir J. C. & S.

Army Form C. 2118.

WAR DIARY
or
INTELLIGENCE SUMMARY

(Erase heading not required.)

Instructions regarding War Diaries and Intelligence Summaries are contained in F. S. Regs., Part II. and the Staff Manual respectively. Title pages will be prepared in manuscript.

Place	Date	Hour	Summary of Events and Information	Remarks and references to Appendices
LA VALLEE	1918 May 28		X & Y Companies working on Reserve Line 1st System – Z Coy on the front line of 2nd System	
	29		do	
	30		do	
	31		During the month 3 Officers and 90 O.R. joined as reinforcements. Cas. 1 man wounded. 5 wounded accidentally. The Military Medal was awarded to the No 8067 L/Corporal F Gallant Clinton to HQ 20 inst when he had been severely wounded.	
	31		Strength: 30 Officers – 517 O.R.	

M Marche Lt Col
Comd 2/4 West Yorkshire Regiment
(Forces)

Army Form C. 2118.

21 W York Regt
Vol 2 6

WAR DIARY
or
INTELLIGENCE SUMMARY
(Erase heading not required.)

Instructions regarding War Diaries and Intelligence Summaries are contained in F. S. Regs., Part II. and the Staff Manual respectively. Title pages will be prepared in manuscript.

Place	Date	Hour	Summary of Events and Information	Remarks and references to Appendices
LA VALLEE	1918 Sept 1.		Strength 30 Officers 517 O.R.	
		1.	X and Y Companies resting, trench boring and improving Reserve line of 1st System.	
		2.	Z Coy the same work in front line of 2nd System.	
		3.	do	
		4.	do	
		5.	do	
		6.	Major Mitchell Comdg. XIII Corps, presented to Military Medal to Sgt Kelly, Pte LEDDER, L/Cpl SMITH and also A.O.M. to C.Q.M.S. HARVEY.	
		7.	do	
		8.	do	
		9.	do	
		10.	do	
		11.	do	
		12.	do Cas: 2 Other X Coy Wounded.	
			Cas: 1 other Z Coy wounded.	

Army Form C. 2118.

WAR DIARY
or
INTELLIGENCE/SUMMARY.
(Erase heading not required.)

Instructions regarding War Diaries and Intelligence Summaries are contained in F. S. Regs., Part II. and the Staff Manual respectively. Title pages will be prepared in manuscript.

Place	Date	Hour	Summary of Events and Information	Remarks and references to Appendices
LA VALLÉE	June 13		X and Y Companies continued on Reserve line 1st System – Z Coy Front line 2nd System.	
	14		do	
	15		do	
	16		do Cas: 2 men Z Coy wounded.	
	17		do Cas: 1 man Y Coy wounded.	
	18		do	
	19		do	
	20		do Cas: 1 man wounded.	
	21		do	
	22		do	
	23		do Cas: 2 men Z wounded.	
	24		do	
	25		do	
	26		do	
	27		do Cas. 1 man Z wounded.	

WAR DIARY
or
INTELLIGENCE SUMMARY
(Erase heading not required.)

Army Form C. 2118.

Place	Date	Hour	Summary of Events and Information	Remarks and references to Appendices
	1918			
LA VALLÉE	June 28		X and Y Companies with continued in Reserve here. 1 Z system Z Co.	
			" " " Front line, 2nd system -	
	29		" " " Casualties: 1 man wounded Z Co.	
	30		" " " " 1 man wounded Z Co.	
			On the King's Birthday Honours list the following award appeared:-	
			Capt. NOBLE, M.C.; Serjts H. BROOKS and HANSON, Pte's MEAD and JORDAN Military Medals: Lt HANSON, Qr M HALL and MILNER, mentions — During the latter half of the month the Battalion suffered from the Epidemic of "Influenza Fever" prevalent in the Division. The total number of cases now 10 Officers and 180 O.R. of whom 3 Officers and 57 O.R.	
			had returned to duty by the end of the month -	
June 30			Fighting Strength 26 Officers 443 O.R.	

S.M. Macllaiffe Lt Col
Cons. 2nd West Yorkshire Regiment (Princep)

WAR DIARY
or
INTELLIGENCE SUMMARY.
(Erase heading not required.)

Army Form C. 2118.

21 W York R

Vol 2

Place	Date	Hour	Summary of Events and Information	Remarks and references to Appendices
LA VALLEE	Aug 1918	1	Fighting strength Officers 26 - OR 443	
		2	X and Y Companies working on Reserve line 1st System - Z Coy " " Front line, 2nd System	
		3	do	
		4	do	
		5	do Cas: 1 man wounded Z Coy	
		6	do	
		7	do Cas: 1 man Y Coy; 1 Z Coy; wounded	
		8	do Cas: 1 man 1 man Y Coy wounded.	
		9	do	
		10	do	
		11	do	
		12	do	
		13	X and Y Companies resting and refitting - Z Coy work as before.	
		14	X and Y Companies began conversion of BATTLE TRENCH (Reserve line of 1st System) to Breastwork for wet weather and winter. Z Co as before.	

WAR DIARY
or
INTELLIGENCE SUMMARY.
(Erase heading not required.)

Army Form C. 2118.

Instructions regarding War Diaries and Intelligence Summaries are contained in F. S. Regs., Part II. and the Staff Manual respectively. Title pages will be prepared in manuscript.

Place	Date	Hour	Summary of Events and Information	Remarks and references to Appendices
LA VALLÉE	1918 July 15		Work continued as yesterday	
		16	do	
		17	do	
		18	do	
		19	do	
		20	do	
		21	Z Coy resting and refitting. Cas: 1 Killed 1 wounded Y Co. Lewis Gun Sect.	
		22	Z Coy began DECAUVILLE line 3/4 mile in left Division Boundary to the Support line – 1st System – Cas. 1 man Y Coy Killed –	
		23	Genl. BIRDWOOD cmg 5th Army, visited and approved work –	
		24	Work interrupted by very heavy rain –	
		25	do	
		26	X and Y Companies began work on CREAM TRENCH converting it into a Breastwork and Parados, working in 4 Posts each – Z Coy continued work front line 2d System in PEACOCK TRENCH. Casualty: 1 man Z Coy wounded –	

Army Form C. 2118.

WAR DIARY
or
INTELLIGENCE SUMMARY
(Erase heading not required.)

Instructions regarding War Diaries and Intelligence Summaries are contained in F. S. Regs., Part II. and the Staff Manual respectively. Title pages will be prepared in manuscript.

Place	Date	Hour	Summary of Events and Information	Remarks and references to Appendices
1916. LA VALLEE	July 27		WHK as yesterday	
	28		do	
	29		do	
	30		do	
	31		From 21st to 26th one Platoon of Z Coy. raid a Decauville Tramway for about 1 mile on the left Divisional Boundary forward to support line. Fighting strength: 26 Officers, 566 O.R.	

SW H Clarke Lt Col
Cmd. 2/8 West Yorkshire Regt

WAR DIARY
or
INTELLIGENCE SUMMARY

(Erase heading not required.)

Army Form C. 2118.

Place	Date	Hour	Summary of Events and Information	Remarks and references to Appendices
LA VALLÉE	1918 Aug. 1		Fighting Strength: 26 Officers, 566 OR –	
			X and Y Companies converting CREAM TRENCH to Breastwork and Parados and continuing revetment of BATTLE TRENCH.	
			Z Coy constructing Posts in PEACOCK TRENCH, 1½ line 2? System –	
			Casualties: 4 men X Coy wounded – 1 man Y Coy wounded –	
	2		Work as yesterday – interrupted by heavy rain.	
	3		do	
	4		do	
	5		do	
	6		do	
	7		do	
	8		All Companies employed clearing and repairing Roads following retirement of enemy and advance of our line in direction of PARADIS. Cas. 1 man X Coy wounded.	
	9		do	
	10		do	

WAR DIARY
or
INTELLIGENCE SUMMARY
(Erase heading not required.)

Army Form C. 2118.

Place	Date	Hour	Summary of Events and Information	Remarks and references to Appendices
	1918.			
LA VALLÉE	Aug. 11		All companies cleaning and repairing Roads following advance of the Division to PARADIS.	
	12		do	
	13		do Cas - 1 man X Coy wounded.	
	14		Y Company at work for 10 days. Company training - X & Z as before	
	15		do	
	16		do Cas. 1 man Z wounded	
	17		do	
	18		do	
	19		do	
	20		do	
	21		do	
	22		do	
	23		do all Companies.	
	24		Battalion marched from LA VALLÉE to CARNOMIN CHATELAIN	

Army Form C. 2118.

WAR DIARY
or
INTELLIGENCE SUMMARY.
(Erase heading not required.)

Instructions regarding War Diaries and Intelligence Summaries are contained in F. S. Regs., Part II. and the Staff Manual respectively. Title pages will be prepared in manuscript.

Place	Date	Hour	Summary of Events and Information	Remarks and references to Appendices
CAMBLAIN L'HATELAIN	1918 Aug 25		Battalion moved by rail to FRAMÉCOURT.	
FRAMÉCOURT	26		by march to CAMBLAIN L'ABBÉ	
CAMBLAIN L'ABBÉ	27		Resting	
	28		Battalion moved by Bus into the line E of MONCHY.	
FOSSE FARM	29		All companies cleaning & repairing forward Roads. Onontain; Sgt-MOXON Killed. 2 men wounded. X Coy.	
	30		do 2 men wounded X Coy	
	31		do 2/Lt PRIDMORE Killed - 4 men wounded -	
			During the month 2/Lt TAYLOR and BRAZIER joined the Battn. Fighting strength 31st Augt 21 Officers 522 O.R -	

S/Lt M.Marke Lt Col
(late 21st Westyorkshire Regt
(Pioneers)

T2134. Wt. W708—776. 500000. 4/15. Sir J.C.&S.

21st (S.) PIONEER BATTN. WEST YORKS. REGT.

WAR DIARY
or
INTELLIGENCE SUMMARY.
(Erase heading not required.)

Army Form C. 2118.

21 W. York R

Place	Date	Hour	Summary of Events and Information	Remarks and references to Appendices
FOSSE FARM	Sept 1		Fighting Strength: 21 Officers 522 OR	
	2		All companies employed in forming Ronds - Division took part in attack on Drocourt-Quéant line - Y Company moved up to clean roads following the advance. Cleaned road from ETERPIGNY to DURY. Casualties: 2nd Lieut E. St L. CLARKE wounded -	
	3		Y Coy made track ETERPIGNY to DROCOURT LINE - X Coy, at night, cleaned Road ETERPIGNY to ETAING - Z Coy, at night, cleaned Road DURY to L'ECLUSE. Casualties: Cpl Cooper, Y, killed. Sgt KAYE, Cpl TUNSTALL and 13 men wounded.	
	4		Division moved out to rest - The Battalion marched to 11th Brigade to billets at HERMIN - Relieved in the lines Pioneers of 1st Division.	
HERMIN	5		Rec'd. General MATHESON visited and addressed Batt'n relating Divisional Company training.	
	6		do	
	7		Church Parade and Battalion Sports -	
	8		Company training -	
	9			

Army Form C. 2118.

WAR DIARY
or
INTELLIGENCE SUMMARY.
(Erase heading not required.)

Instructions regarding War Diaries and Intelligence Summaries are contained in F. S. Regs, Part II. and the Staff Manual respectively. Title pages will be prepared in manuscript.

Place	Date	Hour	Summary of Events and Information	Remarks and references to Appendices
	1918			
HERMIN	Sept 10		Company training	
	11		do	
	12		do	
	13		do	
	14		do	
	15		Church Parade	
	16		Company training	
	17		do	
	18		do	
	19		Lt Col CLARKE rejoined and took over command. The Battalion moved by Bus	
FEUCHY	20		Division went into the line — to FEUCHY AREA, relieving Pioneers of 11th Division — All companies at work improving Roads —	
	21		do	
MONCHY LE PREUX	22		do — Moved HD Qrs and Z Co to MONCHY —	
	23		do	
	24		do	

Army Form C. 2118.

WAR DIARY
or
INTELLIGENCE SUMMARY.
(Erase heading not required.)

Instructions regarding War Diaries and Intelligence Summaries are contained in F. S. Regs., Part II. and the Staff Manual respectively. Title pages will be prepared in manuscript.

Place	Date	Hour	Summary of Events and Information	Remarks and references to Appendices.
MONCHY le PREUX	1918 Sept 25		All Companies at work repairing Roads. Cas: 1 man X Coy wounded.	
	26		do	
	27		do	
	26		do	
	29		do	
	30		do	
			Fighting Strength 27 Officers 527 O.R.	
			The following Officers joined as reinforcements 23rd Sept 2/Lieuts Rose, Midgley, Boyd and Mellors. Captain G.C. Pratt.	
			2/Lt A Larke Lt Col Comd. 21st West Yorkshire Regiment (Pioneers)	

21W York Regt P4

WAR DIARY or INTELLIGENCE SUMMARY

Army Form C. 2118.

Place	Date	Hour	Summary of Events and Information	Remarks and references to Appendices
MONCHY LE PREUX.	1918 Oct 1		Fighting strength: 27 Officers: 527 O.R.– All Companies at work repairing Roads in MONCHY area – One Platoon X Coy sent forward to work from DURY on the L'ECLUSE Road –	
	2		Work as above	
	3		do	
	4		do	
	5		do Casualties: 3 men Y Coy Wounded	
	6		Handed over work to Engineer Battalion 1st Canadian Division.	
DAINVILLE.	7		Battalion marched at 6.45 AM to DAINVILLE.	
	8		Rest and cleaning up.	
	9		X Coy Musketry – Y and Z Company training –	
	10		Y Coy Musketry – X and Z Company training –	
BOURLON WOOD.	11		Battalion moved by Bus to BOURLON WOOD. Passed thro' WANCOURT –	
	12		Transport arrived at 4.30 PM	
ESCAUT DOEUVRES.	13		Battalion marched 1 PM to ESCAUTDOEUVRES	
	14		All Companies at work on Roads IWUY and NAVES area – Major General LIPSETT Cmd'g 3rd Division killed while reconnoitring –	

WAR DIARY or INTELLIGENCE SUMMARY

Army Form C. 2118.

Place	Date	Hour	Summary of Events and Information	Remarks and references to Appendices
ESCAUT-ROEUVRES	1918 Oct 15		Work as yesterday.	
	16		do	
	17		do	
NAVES	18		Battalion moved at 9 am to NAVES taking over work of Pioneers 4½ Div.	
	19		Companies working on roads NAVES – VILLERS : RIEUX – IWUY : VILLERS – IWUY.	
	20		X Coy working on Bridge over River SELLE at SAULZOIR. Y and Z on Roads.	
	21		Y Company began slab road crossing at SAULZOIR Station to divert main road from Bridge over deep cutting. Blown up.	
	22		Work as above. Casualties: 6 men wounded (2 Lieutenants)	
	23		do 2 men wounded.	
	24		Y Coy as above. X Coy clearing main road forward SAULZOIR to VERCHAIN. Z Coy clearing ? HASPRES to MONCHEAUX. Chenelle, Brinewounded following up in advance.	
HASPRES	25		Battalion moved, X Coy and Z Coy to HASPRES. X and Y Companies to SAULZOIR. Advance continued and roads cleared forward up to QUÉRÉNAIN and ? Casualty: 1 man wounded.	
	26		Advance continued and Bridgehead secured over RHONELLE at ARTRES. Work as above.	

WAR DIARY
or
INTELLIGENCE SUMMARY.
(Erase heading not required.)

Army Form C. 2118.

Place	Date	Hour	Summary of Events and Information	Remarks and references to Appendices
HASPRES	1918 Oct 27		X Coy moved SAULZOIR to VERCHAIN — Z Coy, HASPRES to MONCHAUX. Y Coy still making S/W Road at SAULZOIR Station — X and Z clearing roads forward to LA TAPAGE. Cas: Lieut JENKINS wounded.	
	28		Work as above. Cas: 1 man wounded.	
	29		do	
	30		do. Y Coy completed work at SAULZOIR clearing roads forward to ARTRES — Cas: 1 man wounded.	
	31		All Companies employed in roads East of VERCHAIN up to RITONELLE River at ARTRES.	
Fighting Strength			31st Oct. 26 Officers 482 O.R.	

L.M. Clarke Lt Col
Cmdg 21st (S)(Pioneer) Bn
West Yorkshire Regiment.

WAR DIARY or INTELLIGENCE SUMMARY

Army Form C. 2118.

21 November 1918

Place	Date	Hour	Summary of Events and Information	Remarks and references to Appendices
HASPRES	1918 Nov 1		Division attacked from line of River RHONELLE and captured PRESEAU, but lost the Rhonelle in a counterattack X and Z Companies at work keeping roads passable and across the River RHONELLE. Y Coy maintaining the Road VERCHAIN – QUÉRÉNAING. Casualties X Coy: 3 killed 5 wounded, Y 1 man wounded, Z 1 man killed + 9 NCO's and 5 men wounded. Shelling on the roads and heavy and in the village of ARTRES very heavy.	
SAULZOIR	2		Battalion moved to SAULZOIR in afternoon in relief of Pioneers of 11th Div. Work continued as yesterday, into PRESEAU.	
	3		Took over new work QUÉRÉNAING to LETAPE and FAMARS, about 6 miles from Billets.	
	4		Work as yesterday. Moved X and Y Companies to VERCHAIN to be nearer the work.	
ARTRES	5		Battalion moved to ARTRES and took up work on roads East of LÉTAPAGE through ARTRES to PRESEAU.	
	6		As above.	

Army Form C. 2118.

WAR DIARY
or
INTELLIGENCE SUMMARY.
(Erase heading not required.)

Instructions regarding War Diaries and Intelligence Summaries are contained in F. S. Regs., Part II. and the Staff Manual respectively. Title pages will be prepared in manuscript.

Place	Date	Hour	Summary of Events and Information	Remarks and references to Appendices
ARTRES	1918 NOV 7		Work continued as yesterday	
	8		do	
LE TRIEZ	9		Battalion moved to LE TRIEZ.	
	10		Work on roads near LE TRIEZ.	
	11		Companies moved to new work, X to MONTIGNIES; Y to ERQUENNES; Z to ONNEZIES. Armistice signed. Cease fire at 11 A.M.	
	12		Work as above	
	13		do	
	14		do	
	15		do	
	16		do	
	17		do	
	18		X and Y Companies rejoined H.Qrs at LE TRIEZ	
PRÉSEAU	19		Battalion moved to PRÉSEAU.	
	20		Rest and work in new Billets	
	21		do	

Army Form C. 2118.

WAR DIARY
or
INTELLIGENCE SUMMARY.
(Erase heading not required.)

Instructions regarding War Diaries and Intelligence Summaries are contained in F.S. Regs., Part II. and the Staff Manual respectively. Title pages will be prepared in manuscript.

Place	Date	Hour	Summary of Events and Information	Remarks and references to Appendices
PRESEAU	1918 Nov 22		Training - Education - Sports -	
	23		do	
	24		do	
	25		do	
	26		do	
	27		do	
	28		Divisional Parade for Inspection by General Horne. Com'd 1st Army -	
	29		Training - Education - Sports -	
	30		do	
			Fighting Strength: Officers 31. O.R. 469	

E.M.T. Clarke Lt Col
Com'd 21st West Yorkshire Reg'.
(Pioneers)

WAR DIARY or INTELLIGENCE SUMMARY

Army Form C. 2118.

21/W

Place	Date	Hour	Summary of Events and Information	Remarks and references to Appendices
PRESEAU	1918 Dec		Fighting Strength 30 Officers 434 O.R.	
	1		Training Education Sports WR. Divine Service	
	2		2 Coys Training – one Coy (Y) on Salvage work	
	3		Training – Sgt P Leahy died at No 33 C.C.S. (pneumonia)	
	4		Training for X – Y + Z on Salvage work	
	5		Training + Salvage work –	
	6		Target Practice X Coy – Y + Z Kit + Marching Order Inspection	
	7		Training	
	8		Church Parade	
	9		Commanding Officers' Inspections	
	10		Training Education Sports	
	11		do	
	12		Route March Education	
	13		Training Education Sports	1 OR Demobilised
	14		do	6 OR "
	15		Church Parade	12 OR "
	16		Route March (Advance + Rear Guard practice)	7 OR "
				2 OR "

Army Form C. 2118.

WAR DIARY
or
INTELLIGENCE SUMMARY.
(Erase heading not required.)

Instructions regarding War Diaries and Intelligence Summaries are contained in F. S. Regs, Part II. and the Staff Manual respectively. Title pages will be prepared in manuscript.

Place	Date	Hour	Summary of Events and Information	Remarks and references to Appendices
	1918			
PRÉSEAU	Dec 17		Training Education Sports	2 OR Demobed
	18		do do do	8 OR "
	19		do do do	
	20		do do do	
	21		do do do Sgt W. Hirst awarded Military Medal	
	22		Church Parade	
	23		Training Education Sports	1 OR "
	24		Maj Sir S.H.B. Clarke Bart D.S.O. relinquishes Command on Demobilisation - Major	1 Off: "
			W. L. TRENCH assumes Command -	
	25		Church Parade	2 OR "
	26		Holiday - Sports -	
	27		Route March	
	28		Training - Education - Sports -	13 OR "
	29		Church Parade	1 OR "
	30		Training - Education - Sports	3 OR "
	31		do do do	

Fighting Strength 28 Offrs. 414 OR.

W. L. Trench Major
Comdg 2¹/₅th West Yorkshire Regt.

WAR DIARY or INTELLIGENCE SUMMARY

Army Form C. 2118.

21 W York Regt Vol 32

Place	Date	Hour	Summary of Events and Information	Remarks and references to Appendices
PRESEAU	1919 Jan 1		Fighting Strength 28 Officers 414 O.R.	Demob 3 OR
	2		Training Education	" 1 Off —
	3		do	1 w/off + 2 details
	4		Transport moved with 12th Bde to new Area. Billeting party sent	
CHAPELLE LEZ HERLAIMONT (nr CHARLEROI)	5		Bn. moved to CHAPELLE LEZ HERLAIMONT by bus. Transport arr. 17.00 hours	
	6		Arranging Billets	
	7		Training Education	Demob 2 w/Sgts 4 OR
	8		do	Demob 6 OR
	9		do	" 6 OR
	10		do	
	11		Coy/Cdr's Conference. C.O's Inspection	" 1 Off 13 OR
	12		Church Parade	" 12 OR + 1 w/off + details
	13		Training - Party sent to fill in holes dug by enemy at COURCELLES (see 8)	
	14		Training Education	
	15		do	
	16		do	

WAR DIARY or INTELLIGENCE SUMMARY.

(Erase heading not required.)

Army Form C. 2118.

Place	Date	Hour	Summary of Events and Information	Remarks and references to Appendices
	1919			
CHAPELLE LEZ HERLAIMONT (Nr. CHARLEROI)	Jan 17		Training - Education	Demob'd in England 2 O.R.
	18		Coy. Comm'ts Conference C.O's Inspection	
	19		Church Parade	Demob'd 10ff 11 O.R.
	20		Training - Education	Demob'd 2 10ff 12 O.R.
	21		do	Demob'd 2 10ff 11 O.R.
	22		do	
	23		do	
	24		do	
	25		Inspection of Bn. by G.O.C. 4th Div'n at 10.30 hours -	12 O.R.
	26		Church Parade.	12 O.R.
	27		Presentation to the Bn. of the King's Colour by Lieut General Sir A GODLEY, XXII Corps at 12.15 hours. Capt. Brogen the North Sgt Stewart. Mentioned in dispatches. Majr Penn D.S.O. London Gazette 27/12/18	12 O.R. Demob'd 12 O.R. " 15 O.R.
	28, 29		Training - Education -	
	30		Training. Salvage of Ammunition at PONT A CELLES (YEN)	Demob'd 12 O.R.
	31		Training 19 Off's: 307 O.R.	

Fighting Strength

N.L. French M.C.
Comdg. 2/5th Bn. West Yorkshire Regt.

21 W Yorks Rgt

WAR DIARY
or
INTELLIGENCE SUMMARY

Army Form C. 2118.

Vol. 33

(Erase heading not required.)

Instructions regarding War Diaries and Intelligence Summaries are contained in F. S. Regs., Part II. and the Staff Manual respectively. Title pages will be prepared in manuscript.

Place	Date	Hour	Summary of Events and Information	Remarks and references to Appendices
	1919			Demob'ed Off OR
CHAPELLE LEZ HERLAIMONT (nr CHARLEROI)	Feb 1		Fighting Strength 19 Officers 307 OR	— 12
	2		Wol Or SMELLARKE (last DSO mentioned in despatches London Gazette 20/12/18	— 10
	3		Church Parade	— 1
	4		Training – Education – 1 OR demobilised while away from Bn	— 1
	5		MS list 28/1/19 Major WR French MC (late acting Wol); Capt A HARKER MC (late acting Major	— 13
	6		Sgt H Taylor awarded DCM London Gazette 1/1/19 Training – Education	— 11
	7		Training – Education	— 18
	8		do	2 — 17
	9		No Parades	— 6
	10		Voluntary Service	— 1
	11		Training – Education –	— 1
	12		do	— 9
	13		do 5 OR demobilised while away from Bn.	— 7
	14		do	— 8
	15		No Parades 1 OR demobilised while away from Bn	— 13
	16		No Service 2 OR do do	— 14

Army Form C. 2118.

WAR DIARY
or
INTELLIGENCE SUMMARY.
(Erase heading not required.)

Instructions regarding War Diaries and Intelligence Summaries are contained in F. S. Regs., Part II. and the Staff Manual respectively. Title pages will be prepared in manuscript.

Place	Date	Hour	Summary of Events and Information	Remarks and references to Appendices
	1919			Demob^d Off / OR
CHAPELLE LEZ HERLAIMONT (N. CHARLEROI)	Feb. 17		Training Education	— 9
	18		do do Reenlisted OR 4 — 2 OR demobilised while away from Bn	— 6
	19		do do	— 6
	20		do do Reenlisted OR 16	— 12
	21		do do	— 3
	22		No parade	
	23		Church Parade	
	24		Training Education	
	25		do do	
	26		do do Reenlisted OR. 11	— 9
	27		do do 1 OR demobilised while away from bn	— 10
	28		do do Y & Z Coys amalgamated	— 12
			Fighting Strength 22 Officers 266 O.R.	

N.K. French Lt.Col.
Comdg 2nd/8th West Yorkshire Regt.

4 DIVISION. TROOPS.

4 BN MACHINE GUN CORP[S]
1918 MAR TO 1919 FEB

234 MACHINE GUN COMPAN[Y]
1917 JULY TO 1918 FEB.

21 BN WEST YORKSHIRE RE[GT]
(PIONEERS)
1916 JAN TO 1919 FEB.

1472

4 DIVISION. TROOPS.

4 BN MACHINE GUN CORPS
1918 MAR TO 1919 FEB

234 MACHINE GUN COMPANY
1917 JULY TO 1918 FEB.

21 BN WEST YORKSHIRE REGT (PIONEERS)
1916 JAN TO 1919 FEB.

www.ingramcontent.com/pod-product-compliance
Lightning Source LLC
Chambersburg PA
CBHW081431160426
43193CB00013B/2253